THE STRENGTH AND WEAKNESS OF COMPARATIVE LAW

The Strength and Weakness of Comparative Law

BERNHARD GROSSFELD
Professor, University of Münster

translated by
TONY WEIR

Fellow of Trinity College, Cambridge

CLARENDON PRESS · OXFORD
1990

Oxford University Press, Walton Street, Oxford OX2 6DP
Oxford New York Toronto
Delhi Bombay Calcutta Madras Karachi
Petaling Jaya Singapore Hong Kong Tokyo
Nairobi Dar es Salaam Cape Town
Melbourne Auckland
and associated companies in
Berlin Ibadan

Oxford is a trade mark of Oxford University Press

Published in the United States
by Oxford University Press, New York

British Library Cataloguing in Publication Data
Grossfeld, Bernhard,
The strength and weakness of comparative law.
1. Law.
I. Title
340
ISBN 0-19-825256-0

Library of Congress Cataloging in Publication Data
Grossfeld, Bernhard.
[Macht und Ohnmacht der Rechtsvergleichung. English]
The strength and weakness of comparative law / Bernhard Grossfeld; translated by Tony Weir.
Translation of: Macht und Ohnmacht der Rechtsvergleichung.
Includes bibliographical references.
1. Comparative law. I. Title.
K559.G7613 1990 340'.2—dc20 [342] 89-24023
ISBN 0-19-825256-0

Set by Oxford Text System
Printed in Great Britain by
Bookcraft Ltd.,
Midsomer Norton, Avon

Preface

Originating in an attempt to show German lawyers the practical utility (the 'strength') of comparative law, this little book ends up considering some of the central issues of that discipline. The stimulus came in 1979 when I spent several months in Cambridge, England, as Visiting Fellow at Wolfson College, for that sojourn made clear to me how integral a part of a nation's whole culture its law is. A longer stay in Dallas, Texas, as Visiting Professor at Southern Methodist University, enabled me to sense the differences between European and American legal cultures. It was no easy matter—this is the 'weakness' of comparative law—to synthesize such a plethora of different impressions. Whether or not I succeeded, the aim of this book is to set comparative law in the context of the connections between law and general culture.

I am grateful to my hosts in Cambridge and Dallas for such stimulation. Particular thanks are due to John Morrison, Kurt Lipstein, Joseph Norton, Jeswald Salacuse, and Paul Rogers. In Dallas my conversational sparring partner in comparative law was William Bridge; Joseph McKnight greatly assisted me in the chapter 'Geography and Law'; and I could never have embarked on 'Language and Law' without the support of Matthew Finkin and Peter Winship.

For this English version of the book Tony Weir is responsible. It has benefited much from his knowledge of comparative law and of the English and American legal systems, and I am grateful to him for his sympathetic understanding and verbal facility.

Münster
October 1989

B.G.

Contents

Abbreviations

A.B.A.J.	*American Bar Association Journal*
ACP	*Archiv für die civilistische Praxis*
ALR	Allgemeines Landrecht (Prussia)
BFH	Bundesfinanzhof
BGB	Bürgerliches Gesetzbuch
BGE	Decisions of the (Swiss) Bundesgericht
BGH	Bundesgerichtshof
BGHZ	Decisions of the Bundesgerichtshof
BStBl	*Bundessteuerblatt*
BVerfG	Bundesverfassungsgericht
BVerfGE	Decisions of the Bundesverfassungsgericht
FAZ	*Frankfurter Allgemeine Zeitung*
HGB	Handelsgesetzbuch
I.C.L.Q.	*International and Comparative Law Quarterly*
Int.Enc.Comp.Law	*International Encyclopedia of Comparative Law*
IPRax	Praxis des Internationalen Privat- und Verfahrensrecht
IPRspr	Rechtsprechung des Internationalen Privatrechts
JZ	*Juristenzeitung*
N.I.L.Q.	*Northern Ireland Law Quarterly*
NJW	*Neue Juristische Wochenschrift*
OED	*Oxford English Dictionary*
RabelsZ	*Zeitschrift für ausländisches und internationales Privatrecht*
rev.dr.int.dr.comp.	*Revue de droit international et de droit comparé*
rev.int.dr.comp.	*Revue internationale de droit comparé*

RIW	*Recht der Internationalen Wirtschaft, Aussenwirtschaftsdienst des Betriebsberaters*
StGB	Strafgesetzbuch
StPO	Strafprozessordnung
Sw.L.J.	*Southwestern Law Journal*
U.C.L.A.L.R.	*University of California at Los Angeles Law Review*
ZfRV	*Zeitschrift für Rechtsvergleichung* (*Austria*)
ZPO	Zivilprozessordnung
ZSR	*Zeitschrift für schweizerisches Recht*
ZVglRW	*Zeitschrift für Vergleichende Rechtswissenschaft*

1

Introduction

'The Strength and Weakness of Comparative Law' is certainly a theme with many facets. The first question it will raise in the mind of the practising lawyer is 'What contribution has comparative law made to German law, what contribution can it yet make, and in what areas?' The comparative lawyer may well find such a question intimidating, for it forces him to justify not only his own utility to the system but also that of his whole profession.[1] What has comparative law got to offer? Is it even an 'instrument auxiliaire', an ancillary science?[2]

It may be all right for the comparatist who can point, by way of justification, to a great pile of opinions he has written on points of foreign law, but the question is especially hard for one who is quite content that comparative law be an intellectual adventure[3] redolent of the 'magic of jurisprudence',[4] awakening our yearning for distant lands and affording us, like the itinerant craftsmen of old, some spiritual *Wanderjahre*.[5]

[1] On the uses of comparative law see Zweigert & Kötz, 1 *Introduction to Comparative Law* 12 (2nd edn., Oxford, 1987). On the development of comparative law see Zajtay, 'Réflexions sur l'évolution du droit comparé', *Festschrift Zweigert* 595 (Tübingen, 1981); Ancel, 'Valeur actuelle des études de droit comparé', *XXth Century Comparative and Conflicts Law: Essays in Honor of Hessel E. Yntema* 15 (Leiden, 1961); Ancel, 'Cent ans de droit comparé en France', *Livre du centenaire de la société de législation comparée* 1 (Paris, 1969).

[2] See Genzmer, 'A Civil Lawyer's Critical Views on Comparative Legal History', 15 *Am.J.Comp.L.* 87 (1967); Wagner, 'Research in Comparative Law: Some Theoretical Considerations', in Newman (ed.), *Essays in Jurisprudence in Honor of Roscoe Pound* 511 (Indianapolis, 1962).

[3] Cardozo, 'Values: The Choice of Tycho Brahe', in *Selected Writings of Benjamin Cardozo* 1 (New York, 1947); Holmes, 'Law in Science and Science in Law', in Henson, *Landmarks of Law* 229, 230 (Boston, 1960): 'It is perfectly proper to regard and study the law simply as a great anthropological document'; Wagner (above n. 2) 526.

[4] See Buckmester, 'The Romance of the Law', in Henson (above n. 3) 451.

[5] Lawson, 'Comparative Law, Instrument of Legal Culture', in Lawson, 2 *Many Laws: Selected Essays* 68 (Amsterdam, 1977).

As a means of extending our mental horizons, comparative law can be easily and amply justified. Rudolf von Jhering can be the leading witness: 'Legal science has become provincial, scholarship confined within political boundaries. This is a wretched and unseemly state for any science.'[6]

From this point of view it is easy to fault the present state of legal education as regards comparative law. It is not just a question of the numbers of lectures or chairs, of improving the statistics. The trouble is that German legal education has become horribly provincial—'horribly' is none too strong a word in the view of comparative lawyers—concentrating almost exclusively on problems of municipal law. In a legal system with international dimensions (European Community, United Nations) this is a grave defect, and the lawyers we turn out, despite their unduly long training, are not properly equipped to cope with international intercourse, not really a match for the foreign competition.

This is not so much because they do not know enough foreign law—after all, we can hardly stuff any more data into youngsters already condemned to too many years of mere absorption. It is because foreign orientation or experience get you no credit from the examiners. As Gamillscheg said recently: 'If students invested in foreign languages the time they spend plumbing the depths of §812 or §987 BGB they would be better equipped for their professional career.'[7]

But present circumstances are unpropitious. To do well in the examinations one must be highly proficient in the technicalities of national law;[8] the 'wise' student is well advised to keep body and mind at home. The international

[6] Von Jhering, 1 *Geist des römischen Rechts auf den verschiedenen Stufen seiner Entwicklung* 15 (10th edn., Aalen, 1968); Pound, 'The Passing of Mainstreetism', in *XXth Century Comparative and Conflicts Law: Essays in Honor of Hessel E. Yntema* 3 (Leiden, 1961).

[7] Gamillscheg, 'Das Werkzeug der Arbeitsrechtsvergleichung', *Festschrift Zweigert* 433 (Tübingen, 1981).

[8] For similar tendencies in the United States see Mentschikoff & Stotzky, *The Theory and Craft of American Law* (New York, 1981); also Martineau, 'Legal Education and Training Artists of the Law', 57 *N.Y.U.L.Rev.* 346 (1982).

challenge gets lost to view. The students are not to be blamed; we should be beating our own breast!

It is much the same when they go into practice. People complain that 'young people' refuse to travel, but when you ask what return they would get from a period abroad, there is often an eloquent silence, especially in firms which, frankly, put image at home before performance abroad. The young people's reaction to our posture is quite rational; after all, 'Youngsters warble what their elders sang'.

This tendency to stick in Germany is all the more serious because the study of German law is becoming less and less attractive to foreigners. What can the foreigner gain from the flood of student books or the mass of specialized doctrine? It is hardly an exportable commodity. The international validity of German legal scholarship is at risk. Maitland said 'We have all of us been nationalists of late. Cosmopolitanism can afford to await its turn,'[9] but before we take comfort from that, we should remember that he said it at the turn of the century. Can we still afford to wait? If we don't seize the opportunities, there are others who will!

But even if one grants the need for comparative law, comparative lawyers still have some persuading to do. Important as it is to stimulate interest and develop initiative, our discipline has stronger claims to scholarship than that. The problem here is of the scientific nature of law, and it is especially acute for comparatists. There is a constant demand for the busywork of comparative law, listing differences, summarizing the law of various countries, and responding to hasty proposals for law reform. In the eighteenth century Justus Möser from Osnabrück had a brusque reaction to a similar phenomenon in another context:

Even the sexton represents the opinion of the elders as a terrible spectre . . . and tells the children that before they can run a farm properly they have to read great tomes and go to school in England

[9] Maitland, 'English Law and the Renaissance', in: 1 *Selected Essays in Anglo-American Legal History* 168, 176 (1907).

or France or Sweden; and he makes proposals which ten generations of experience have shown to be unworkable.[10]

The discipline of comparative law has sometimes come in for severe condemnation. Binder described it as 'making a pile of bricks and then leaving them unused'.[11] Another critic wrote that 'Comparative law often runs the risk of losing its mind in the matter.'[12] The comparative lawyer himself may come in for persiflage, like the joke that he rates as an expert in foreign law when he is at home and as an expert in German law when he is abroad. And to say that comparative law is based on 'intuition'[13] or is 'more of an art than a science'[14] does little to allay scepticism.

All this, understandably enough, engenders a certain reserve about comparative law and its utility. Admittedly no one today would treat foreign law as 'almost ridiculous', as Cicero did,[15] but it was only in 1856 that the General Code of the Canton of Aargau laid down that 'No court may, by way of interpretation or amplification of this Code, base its judgment on any foreign law.'[16] We may perhaps recall that the Prussian General Land Law of 1794 banned even the 'opinions of law teachers'.[17]

Smile as we may, serious questions lurk in the background, questions of formal legality and the rule of law, of judicial

[10] Justus Möser, 'Es bleibt beim Alten', in *Patriotische Phantasien*, 4 *Sämtliche Werke* 183 f. (Oldenburg, n.d.).

[11] Binder, *Philosophie des Rechts* 948 (Berlin, 1925).

[12] Marcus Lutter, 'Vom formellen Mindestkapital zu materiellen Finanzierungsregeln im Recht der Kapitalgesellschaften', *Festschrift Riesenfeld* 165 (Heidelberg, 1983).

[13] Hall, 'Comparative Law as Basic Research', 4 *Hastings Int'l & Comp.L.Rev.* 189, 199 (1980).

[14] Butler, 'International Law and the Comparative Method', 30 *Curr.Leg.Prob.* 105, 106 (1977).

[15] Cicero, *De Oratore* I. 44. 197; compare *Tusculan Disputations* I. 1–2.

[16] In art. 14; see Meier-Hayoz, 1 *Berner Kommentar zum schweizerischen Zivilrecht* Art. 1 no. 361 (Berne, 1962) who also cites art. 3 of the Code civil of the Canton of Vaud: 'Il est défendu aux juges de citer, comme motif de leur jugement, une loi ou une autorité étrangère, pour expliquer le présent code, ou pour y suppléer.'

[17] Prussian Allgemeines Landrecht I §6: 'Decisions henceforth shall take no account of opinions of jurists or prior judicial pronouncements', a formulation criticized by Justus Möser, 'Schreiben eines alten Rechtsgelehrten über das sogenannte Allegiren', in *Patriotische Phantasien* 117 (above n. 10).

freedom, of Montesquieu's remark that it is 'un grand hasard' if the laws of one nation turn out to suit another.[18] To this day the French courts seem very hesitant in this area, though their very distinctive style of writing opinions may contribute to this impression.[19]

Lord Diplock was similarly unenthusiastic quite recently when he said in the House of Lords that it would be inconsistent with the traditional development of the common law of England 'to attempt to incorporate holus bolus from some other system of law . . . doctrines or legal concepts that have hitherto been unrecognised in English common law'. This although the doctrine of *forum non conveniens* of which he was speaking was the *Scottish* one![20]

Much of the opposition to comparative law has been mitigated in recent years by internationalization and cultural exchanges; indeed, 'international euphoria', the heady air of the big wide world, may occasionally induce us to overlook obstacles which still exist. And then new obstacles arise: comparative law can add to the 'deluge of norms' we are always moaning about. Nor can comparative law be content these days with foraging for strictly legal solutions; extra-legal solutions are every bit as important.[21] After all, law is only one of many methods of social adaptation, and a cumbrous, unreliable, and costly one at that.[22] Indeed, it often leaves the problems unsolved.

[18] Montesquieu, 1 *De l'esprit des lois* 10 (Des lois positives) (ed. Truc, Paris, 1956): 'Les lois politiques et civiles de chaque nation . . . doivent être tellement propres au peuple pour lequel elles sont faites, que c'est un grand hasard si celles d'une nation peuvent convenir à une autre.'

[19] Rolland, 'La magistrature française devant le droit comparé', in *Livre du centenaire de la société de législation comparée* 341, 351 (Paris, 1969); Esmein, 'Le droit comparé et l'enseignement du droit', [1899 1900] Bulletin de la société de législation comparée 376. See too Saleilles, 'Le code civil et la méthode historique', in 1 *Le Code civil, Livre du centenaire* 95, 127 n. 3 (Paris, 1904).

[20] *McShannon* v. *Rockware Glass Ltd.* [1978] A.C. 795, 811. Later, however, Lord Diplock said that 'judicial chauvinism has been replaced by judicial comity to an extent which . . . is . . . indistinguishable from the Scottish legal doctrine of forum non conveniens.' *The Abidin Daver* [1984] 1 All E.R. 470, 476.

[21] See Kim & Lawson, 'The Law of the Subtle Mind: The Traditional Japanese Conception of Law', 28 *I.C.L.Q.* 491, 501 (1979).

[22] Kahn-Freund, 'English Law and American Law: Some Comparative Reflexions', in Newman (ed.), *Essays in Jurisprudence in Honor of Roscoe Pound* 362, 407 (Indianapolis, 1962).

Current views about the utility of comparative law range very widely. One scholar praises it as a 'universal method of interpretation' while another speaks of 'the law of the non-transferability of law'.[23] Perhaps they have different kinds of comparative law in mind, one looking to the cultures of the West, and the other including Africa and Asia. The down-to-earth commonsensical practical lawyer doubtless feels more comfortable somewhere between the two positions. Of course, it all depends. Yes, indeed; but what does it all depend on?

[23] Hiller, 'Language, Law, Sports and Culture: The Transferability of Words, Lifestyles and Attitudes through Law', 12 *Valparaiso U.L.Rev.* 433 (1978); Wroblewski, 'Problems of Incomparability in Comparative Law', 53 *Riv.int. di filosofia di diritto* 92 (1976).

2

Comparative Law, Legal Doctrine, and Law in Practice

If comparative law as such presents difficulties, our theme presents others, for its very terms are uncertain. Take the word 'strength', for example. Does this suggest cause and effect, influence? If so, how strong must an influence be to count as a 'contribution'?[1] This is no mere play with words. For all that comparative law is part of our cultural environment today and often forms the climate of discourse, it is very hard to ascertain its precise effect. Again, comparative law makes its mark on the personality of its adepts: the comparatist has seen the world, figuratively speaking, he has a different approach to legal questions, perhaps even an altered awareness of law. One does not have to believe in the existence of 'legal grandees' or 'key figures'[2] in order to recognize how greatly a legal culture depends on the education and personality of its lawyers, and to realize what an influence comparative law is bound to have. German lawyers should be especially conscious of the influence of individuals, seeing what contributions their compatriots of a previous generation made in the countries in which they took refuge.[3] In what follows, however, I shall be concentrating mainly on technical-juridical influences.

Then after the Scylla of 'strength' comes the Charybdis of 'comparative law'. What *is* comparative law? The component 'law' is enigmatic enough, but let us leave that aside and

[1] See Jackson, 'Evolution and Foreign Influence in Ancient Law', 16 *Am.J.Comp.L.* 373 (1968): 'Influence has become almost a dirty word in legal history.'

[2] See Rheinstein, 'Die Rechtshonoratioren und ihr Einfluss auf Charakter und Funktion der Rechtsordnungen', 34 *RabelsZ* 1 (1970); Bernstein, 'Rechtsstile und Rechtshonoratioren', ibid. 443.

[3] Touster, 'Reflections on the Émigré Scholar: In Memory of Arthur Lenhoff', 16 *Buffalo L.Rev.* 1 (1966).

consider 'comparative law' as a whole. Here controversy abounds; there is no generally accepted theoretical framework; the concept, its aims, its object, and its method are all in issue.[4] If we waited for clarification, we would never get down to business.

If one takes comparative law to be the comparison of legal cultures, which is the only sensible way to treat it,[5] it is hard to distinguish it from other methods of acquiring experience of foreign affairs. Suppose one goes to the United States to find out about clinical legal education, so important in a country where all legal training is done in law-school, is that comparative law? Which currently fashionable ideas belong to comparative law? How do we decide? What about 'emancipation', 'anti-authoritarian upbringing', 'the welfare of the child', 'consumer protection', 'protection of the environment', 'critical legal studies', 'the Swedish model'? These ideas do more to change the law than anything comparative lawyers can do, for comparative law often trails behind such ideas or jumps on their bandwagon. This demonstrates the limits of comparative law as a calling, marks out the boundaries of our discipline: it is an important factor in denationalizing our legal culture, but not the most important one.

The next question is, what exactly do practitioners of comparative law actually compare? What is the object of our specialty? What have we in mind when we speak of German or Chinese 'law'?[6] Are we to include extra-legal rules?[7] Indeed we must, or our picture of the foreign legal system will be

[4] Kamba, 'Comparative Law: A Theoretical Framework', 23 *I.C.L.Q.* 485 (1974); McDougal, 'The Comparative Study of Law for Policy Purposes: Value Clarification as an Instrument of Democratic World Order', 1 *Am.J.Comp.L.* 24 (1952). Gutteridge, *Comparative Law* (2nd edn., Cambridge, 1949), is still well worth reading.

[5] Ehrmann, *Comparative Legal Cultures* (Englewood Cliffs, 1976).

[6] See Merryman & Clark, *Western European and Latin American Legal Systems* 27 (Indianapolis, 1978); Pound, 'What Constitutes Good Legal Education?', 19 *A.B.A.J.* 627 (1933); Banakas, 'Some Thoughts on the Method of Comparative Law: The Concept of Law Revisited', 67 *Archiv für Rechts- und Sozialphilosophie* 289 (1981).

[7] Bohannan, 'Law and Legal Institutions', in Evan (ed.), *The Sociology of Law* 3 (New York, 1980).

sadly distorted. Often the thing that 'goes without saying', that remains unspoken, never questioned, has a greater impact than what we call law. So, too, there are taboos, conscious or unconscious. Law is only the tip of the iceberg.

How are we to respond to a system which is not habituated to 'law' in our sense,[8] where court decision is not the model method of resolving disputes?[9] We have no intercultural notion of 'law':[10] our rather formal conception of it is culturally determined.[11] Other peoples see any authoritative pronouncement as 'law', that is, as a rule to be followed, though it may be a question what counts as an authority. The deep structure is often not what we think it and is not to be found where we look for it. The trouble is that we see other cultures through preconceptions from our own. Perhaps we cannot do otherwise. But this leads to problems of method which we cannot deal with here. One may just mention 'functional comparative law',[12] 'economic analysis of law', and 'sociological aspects'.

Let me be a little more specific about 'German law' and focus on the use in private and business law of legal doctrine, the formal approach to legal thinking, black-letter law, what I shall here call 'conceptualism'. The notion, vague as it is, has negative overtones, but I must declare an interest. A lot of people think that it is a terrible thing to be a conceptualist; they speak, more perhaps from wishful thinking than sober analysis, of the 'crisis of conceptualism'. I plead guilty to being a conceptualist, terrible though it may be. The notion of conceptualism is a kaleidoscopic one, because law itself is kaleidoscopic. By 'conceptualism' I understand at least a

[8] Victor H. Li, *Law Without Lawyers* (Boulder, 1978); Noda, 'The Far Eastern Conception of Law', in 2 *Int.Enc.Comp.Law* 120 (Tübingen, 1973); Chin Kim, *Selected Writings on Asian Law* (Littleton, Colo., 1982).

[9] Abel, *The Politics of Informal Justice* (New York, 1982).

[10] See Pospisil, *Anthropology of Law* (New York, 1971).

[11] See Herget, 'Shaking Loose from an Old Jurisprudence: What is the Price?', 36 *Sw.L.J.* 807 (1982); Sawer, 'The Western Conception of Law', in 2 *Int.Enc.Comp.Law* 10 (Tübingen, 1973).

[12] See Folke Schmidt, 'The Need for a Multi-Axial Method in Comparative Law', *Festschrift Zweigert* 525 (Tübingen, 1981).

concern for the inner harmony of the legal system and the elucidation of the way its elements cohere. The function of conceptualism is 'to reveal the basic interconnections of the legal ideas on which the legal system rests'.[13] At the same time conceptualism is an epitome of everything lawyers have learnt through the ages and a link with juridical tradition. But more than anything else it is a means of rationalizing decisions. It is the legal version of that principle of economy which is so striking a feature of European social and intellectual history, a principle to which I am greatly attached. Furthermore, conceptualism assists in rendering justice systematic, as is indeed required by the very principle of equality.

Conceptualism renders the legal system perspicuous and intelligible (as the rule of law requires), and meets our need for precise language and sharp ideation. Its disciplinary effect upon lawyers is a further advantage. It is true that 'it is harder to break out of a framework of systematic thought than to range freely in the open',[14] but the effort generates new strength.

But then a serious problem arises: how can comparative law and conceptualism be reconciled? Are they not fire and water, diametrically opposed methods? Can the study of foreign law teach us anything about the internal consistency of our own law, about its inner harmonies? Many are dubious, including Zweigert, who, along with Constantinesco and after Rabel, has done so much for comparative law in our country. In Zweigert's view comparative law is anti-conceptualistic by its very nature, and he is quite severe and uncompromising in saying:

> Working in comparative law gives one new grounds for scepticism about conceptualism in law. The dogmatic and the functional are two different methods of thinking about law, or rather different stages in the development of legal science. And one may ask

[13] Mayer-Maly, *Rechtswissenschaft* 8 (2nd edn., Munich, 1981).

[14] Dölle, 'Rechtsdogmatik und Rechtsvergleichung', 34 *RabelsZ* 409 (1970).

how legal concepts and doctrine can possibly assist functional jurisprudence.[15]

This really amounts to a judgement, on the basis of comparative law, that conceptualism is historically obsolete.

Rabel's view was rather different: comparative law can free 'the kernel of legal phenomena from the husk of their formulae and superstructures and [maintain] the coherence of a common legal culture'.[16] Comparative law can certainly help us to elicit the essentials of our own law. Thus Dölle has insisted that comparative law can help us to see systematic and doctrinal solutions. Comparative law is then not in competition with conceptualism but in partnership with it. Constantinesco is more specific. Comparative law can expose any oversophistication or imprecision in legal doctrine; it can confirm or confute doctrinal principles and postulates; it thus exercises a control function: 'Comparative law sharpens the eye for defects and weaknesses in one's national legal institutions. The comparatist can bring to bear on his home system a judgment which is more mature, thanks to his wider experience, and more critical, thanks to his deeper understanding of the matter.'[17]

I entirely agree, and would only add that comparative law can also sharpen one's appreciation of the value of conceptualism. It took a conversation with Rheinstein in Chicago to make me realize what a tremendous legacy we Germans had received from nineteenth-century scholarship in law. One only has to see what trouble has resulted from the abandonment of conceptual thinking in the United States, and how costly it is proving.[18] Progress, indeed!

But this 'either-or' approach to method is something I

[15] Zweigert, ' "Rechtsgeschäfte" und "Vertrag" heute', 2 *Festschrift Rheinstein* 493 ff. (Tübingen, 1969).

[16] Cited by Coing, 'Das Deutsche Schuldrecht und die Rechtsvergleichung', 1956 *NJW* 569, 570.

[17] Constantinesco, 2 *Rechtsvergleichung: Die rechtsvergleichende Methode* 335 (Cologne, 1972).

[18] See *Re Air Crash Disaster near Chicago*, 644 F.2d 594 (7th Cir. 1981); Fawcett, 'Is American Governmental Interest Analysis the Solution to English Tort Choice of Law Problems?', 31 *I.C.L.Q.* 150 (1982).

have never been able to understand; our specialty is surely too large for one method to be enough; it is hardly the place for a monopoly. Even logic and experience are not, as it seems to me, so sharply opposed as Holmes suggests when he says that 'The life of law is not logic but experience'.[19] Striking as this apophthegm is, it must be seen in the light of the special need for pragmatism in the United States; too much may be read into it if it is severed from its local origins. The role of logic in law depends on subjective and objective stability, a point on which there are differences between the Americans and ourselves.

This applies, I think, to comparative law and conceptualism. A conceptual framework is useful, for it often makes it easier for the comparatist to find the right question to ask. It is a well-established rule of comparative law that one should start by a clear analysis of one's own law before proceeding to think comparatively. But we also need comparative law as a stimulant, as a protection against the ormolu of doctrine, as an escape from the occasional oversophistication. It tunes us in to other systems, and saves us from nationalistic narcissism.

So far so good. But is comparative law *appropriate* in the realm of doctrine? Is anything to be gained, for example, by comparing our principle of abstract conveyance with the French doctrine of *cause*? Zweigert says that 'inner structural connections' set a limit to the use of comparative law as a method of interpretation, just as the clear words of a statute may do. But our example of the principle of abstraction suggests a different answer. Comparative law enables us to see the true worth and value of this principle, both its avowed aim—the protection of commerce—and its unintended effect—the protection of the transferee's creditors, both the weight it can bear and its proper scope.

For the application of law we must turn to the practice of the courts. Here comparative law has obvious limitations,

[19] Holmes, *The Common Law* 1 (44th edn., Boston, 1951).

for it has no power to lay down rules, and it has nothing to say of direct use to the decision-maker. Apart from certain areas of conflicts law, it can help only where our law is 'open', where there is room for interpretation. But where there is any such room, comparative law can and should be used, with all due caution. This is not without its problems, as has already been indicated, for comparative law may open the door to foreign views unenvisaged by the legislator.

But here comparative law can pull itself up by its own bootstraps. The Swiss Civil Code comes to our aid: 'If there is no relevant provision in the Code, the judge is to decide in accordance with customary law, if any, or in accordance with the rule he would adopt if he were the legislator, taking due account of doctrine and tradition' (Art. 1 par. 2). Meier-Hayoz draws this conclusion: 'Since the federal legislator uses the comparative method, the judge must use it too, for when there is any gap to be filled he is to proceed as the legislator would.'[20] Swiss courts have therefore had no hesitation in invoking foreign law.[21] They treat comparative law as 'an auxiliary source of law which is recognized today by scholars and practitioners'.[22] Similar conclusions are reached in Austria on the basis of §7 ABGB and the principles of natural law which it incorporates by reference.

These instances are cited by Zweigert when he credits comparative law with being a 'universal method of interpretation',[23] and in one of its early decisions the Federal Constitutional Court agreed: 'For the rest, courts have used

[20] Meier-Hayoz, 1 *Berner Kommentar zum schweizerischen Zivilrecht*, Art. 1 no. 368.

[21] Ibid., at nos. 364–366.

[22] Ibid., at no. 366. No. 368 gives the text of art. 7 of the Swiss Carriage by Sea Act: 'If no rule can be found in federal legislation, especially this Act and provisions of international treaties declared applicable, the judge is to decide in accordance with the general principles of sea law, and, in their absence, in accordance with the rule he would adopt were he the legislator, taking account of legislation, customary law, the opinions of scholars and the decisions of courts.'

[23] Zweigert, 'Rechtsvergleichung als universale Interpretationsmethode', 15 *RabelsZ* 5 (1949–50).

the assistance of the established methods of interpretation and gap-filling, as well as comparative law.'[24]

But we must not go too far. Comparative law may be useful in certain circumstances but it is up to the judge to decide whether to use it or not (except perhaps in cases of private international law or unified law).[25] Again, courts cannot do much comparative law on their own, if only for lack of time and adequate library facilities; they usually have to rely on the writings of comparatists. Furthermore, the courts should be cautious in their use of comparative law, except, perhaps, with systems which are closely related. As will be seen, snares and traps abound, and the theory of the 'universal method of interpretation' might induce us to overlook them. It is generally best for comparative law to be filtered through the literature: in this way scholars can play the role in creative jurisprudence in which they are most valuable, namely anticipating the problems of practice and showing the way forward.

[24] BVerfGE 3, 208, 244.
[25] e.g. *Fothergill* v. *Monarch Airlines Ltd.* [1981] A.C. 251; Art. 36 EGBGB.

3

Legislation

Enough of abstract considerations; let us get down to details. Wherein lies the 'strength' of comparative law? The question has often been addressed, by Dölle and Aubin, to mention but two.[1] For French law the *Livre du centenaire de la société de la législation comparée* is an exemplary and comprehensive treatment,[2] and comparable research has been done in Swiss law.[3]

Let us start with the influence of comparative law on legislation, since enacted law dominates the study as well as the courtroom. The influence of comparative law on legislation at the national and international levels has been well researched, and I shall not repeat what others have said about it.[4] The research confirms Zweigert's view that legislators do indeed practise comparative law, if somewhat eclectically.[5] In England statute even requires the Law Commission, whose main function is to propose reforms of the law, 'to obtain such information as to the legal systems

[1] Dölle, 'Der Beitrag der Rechtsvergleichung zum deutschen Recht', in 2 *Hundert Jahre Deutsches Rechtsleben, Festschrift zum hundertjährigen Bestehen des Deutschen Juristentages 1860–1960* 99 (Karlsruhe, 1960); Aubin, 'Die rechtsvergleichende Konkretisierung von Kontrollmassstäben des Verfassungsrechts und des Kollisionsrechts in der deutschen Rechtsprechung', in *Deutsche Landesreferate zum VII. internationalen Kongress für Rechtsvergleichung in Uppsala 1966* (Tübingen, 1967); Aubin, 'Die rechtsvergleichende Interpretation autonominternen Rechts in der deutschen Rechtsprechung', 34 *RabelsZ* 458 (1970).

[2] (Paris, 1969). See also Elkind, *The Impact of American Law on English and Commonwealth Law* (St Paul, 1978).

[3] A. B. Schwarz, *Das schweizerische Zivilgesetzbuch in der ausländischen Rechtsentwicklung* (Zurich, 1970); Siehr, 'Die Zeitschrift für schweizerisches Recht und das schweizerische Privatrecht in der deutschen Rechtspraxis', 100 *ZSR* (I) 51 (1981).

[4] Grünhut, 'English Law and the History of Continental Legislation', 30 *J.Comp.Leg. & Int'l L.* (3rd ser.) 165 (1938).

[5] Zweigert, 'Rechtsvergleichung als universale Interpretationsmethode', 15 *RabelsZ* 5 (1949–50).

of other countries as appears to the Commissioners likely to facilitate the performance of any of their functions.'[6]

Legislators have been making use of comparative law for very many years. For a European example, we may note that the provision of the Treaty of Rome relating to 'trade between Member States' (Art. 85) comes from the interstate commerce clause of the United States Constitution. In German law I shall mention just a few important areas of law.

We have England to thank for our income tax,[7] not just the idea but also the techniques (the concept of 'source', tax declaration, withholding). Income tax was introduced in England by William Pitt in 1798, at a critical stage in the Napoleonic Wars. 'The tax that beat Napoleon' came to Prussia through Königsberg, seat of the Prussian Court after the Peace of Tilsit, and Prussian law remained under the influence of the English Income Tax Act, 1842, right up till 1891, when Johannes von Miquel introduced his reforms. Miquel was born in the Kingdom of Hanover, in the county of Bentheim, studied in Göttingen, and first worked in Osnabrück. This is significant because under the personal union of the crowns Göttingen University and the Kingdom of Hanover were the ports of entry into Germany for English thinking. Many of the Prussian reformers, such as von Stein, were influenced by English thought, especially that of Adam Smith, and almost all were alumni of Göttingen.

This western influence on tax law continued. Our doctrine of proper allowances for dealings between connected enterprises reflects that of the Internal Revenue Code of the United States (§482); American principles also underlie the way we tax foreign earnings.

Then there is company law. The earliest legislation on

[6] Law Commissions Act 1965, s. 3(1)(f). Marsh, 'Comparative Law and Law Reform', 41 *RabelsZ* 649 (1977); Stein, 'Uses, Misuses and Non-uses of Comparative Law', 72 *Nw.U.L.Rev.* 198, 209 (1977); van Dunné, 'The Use of Comparative Law by the Legislator in the Netherlands', *Netherlands Report to the Eleventh International Congress on Comparative Law* 37 (1983).

[7] Grossfeld & Bryce, 'A Brief Comparative History of the Origins of the Income Tax in Great Britain, Germany and the United States', 2 *Am.J.Tax Policy* 211 (1983).

companies was the Code de Commerce of 1807, enacting the charter system. This formed the basis of the Prussian Company Law of 1843.[8] The replacement of the system of state charters by free incorporation in 1870 was indubitably due to prior developments in France and England. Comparative law has continued to be a force in this area, as witness the names of Franz Klein,[9] and, for the Reform of 1965, Heinrich Kronstein ('sealed glass boxes').[10]

The contribution of comparative law to the Bankruptcy Ordinance of 1877 is well known: the Preamble emphasizes the assistance obtained from the study of foreign laws, and memoranda on English and American bankruptcy laws are included in an Appendix. The current work of the Commission on Insolvency Law and the plans for a Reorganization Procedure show that comparative law continues to exercise an influence.[11]

Comparative law also led the way in anti-trust law. We have become rather accustomed since the War to treating the United States as the source of anti-trust law, but the roots of our law lie elsewhere. They lie in Austria. Draft laws drawn up there towards the end of the century inspired the first modern German cartel law, the Cartel Ordinance of 1923. The influence here is more clearly traceable than in tax law. Schäffle wrote a report on the Austrian proposals. Graf von Posadowsky-Wehner, the Imperial Home Secretary, read it. Work on an Anti-Trust Law for Germany was put in hand. And if comparative law instigated the enterprise, it also fuelled it, for the *Memorandum on Cartels*,[12] an outstanding piece of work, was the product of comparative studies commissioned by the imperial government, to which a

[8] Von Baums (ed.), *Gesetz über die Aktiengesellschaften für die Königlich-Preussischen Staaten vom 9.11.1843, Text und Materialien* (Aalen, 1981).

[9] Franz Klein, *Die neueren Entwicklungen in Verfassung und Recht der Aktiengesellschaft* (Vienna, 1904), and *Die wirtschaftlichen und sozialen Grundlagen des Rechts der Erwerbsgesellschaften* (Berlin, 1914).

[10] Kronstein & Claussen, *Publizität und Gewinnverteilung im neuen Aktienrecht* (Frankfurt, 1960).

[11] Flessner, *Sanierung und Reorganisation* (Tübingen, 1982).

[12] *Denkschrift über das Kartellwesen* (*mit Anlagen*) (Berlin, 1906).

major contribution was made by Austrian scholars, especially Franz Klein.

The list of examples could be greatly extended. Students know how greatly private law is indebted to Adam Smith's *An Inquiry into the Nature and Causes of the Wealth of Nations* (1776). Many of the ideas in the law of obligations in the BGB are drawn from the Swiss Law of Obligations of 1881, itself based on extensive comparative studies. And our law of civil procedure was heavily influenced by the law of Austria, especially the amendments of 1909, 1924, and 1933. Here, too, the name of Franz Klein crops up. Perhaps, after all, Rheinstein was right and there *are* 'legal grandees'.[13]

Finally I can refer to the part played by comparative law in the proposed legislation on the media, and in the drafting of the Private International Law Act by the German Commission for Private International Law. Mention could also be made of the harmonization and unification of law within the Common Market, which gives comparative law a direct and powerful influence on our law.[14] But perhaps the foremost contribution of comparative law today lies in the unification of law on the international plane (Uniform Sales Law, Law of Accounting) and in international Codes of Conduct.

Some critics object that the legislator's research is sometimes superficial, and that the choice of legal systems for comparison is sometimes arbitrary, depending on the linguistic abilities or personal connections of the reporters. We cannot go into these objections here. It is clear that legislators are open to comparative law, even if the degree of openness may vary from Ministry to Ministry; and that is enough for our purposes.

[13] Rheinstein, 'Die Rechtshonoratioren und ihr Einfluss auf Charakter und Funktion der Rechtsordnung', 34 *RabelsZ* 1 (1970).

[14] Neumayer, 'The Role of Uniform Legal Science in the Harmonisation of the Continental Legal Systems', in Newman (ed.), *Essays in Jurisprudence in Honor of Roscoe Pound* 649 (Indianapolis, 1962).

4

Private International Law

Now we face a devilish question—can comparative law be of use to legal scholarship? If we start with those areas of law which have an international flavour and so are naturally close to comparative law there can be no doubt at all. For public international law[1] and its general principles[2] comparative law is vital. One topical example is the new doctrine of limiting the immunity of sovereign states in commercial matters.[3] The same is true of European law: the Court of the European Communities often bases its opinions on comparative law.[4] So too for any law incorporated in an international treaty: here comparative law can promote unanimity in the first instance, avoid characterization conflicts, and, if kept alive, help to achieve the aims of the treaty. We can see this now in the EEC Convention on Jurisdiction and the Enforcement of Judgments in Civil and Commercial Matters,[5] in the Uniform Law of Sales, and in uniform international law generally. The same will be true of the European Law of Accounting.

The theory of private international law has traditionally been steeped in comparative law.[6] This is quite natural, given that it is an expression of the international legal community

[1] Butler, *International Law in Comparative Perspective* (Alphen an Rijn, 1980); Butler, 'International Law and the Comparative Method', 30 *Curr.Leg.Prob.* 105 (1977).

[2] Schlesinger, 'The Common Core of Legal Systems: An Emerging Subject of Comparative Study', in *XXth Century Comparative and Conflicts Law: Essays in Honor of Hessel E. Yntema* 65 (Leiden, 1961).

[3] BVerfG, RIW 1983, 613.

[4] Lorenz, 'General Principles of Law: Their Elaboration in the Court of Justice of the European Communities', 13 *Am.J.Comp.L.* 1 (1964); Pescatore, 'Droit comparé et jurisprudence de la Cour de Justice des Communautés Européennes, 32 *rev.int.dr.comp.* 337 (1980).

[5] See Civil Jurisdiction & Judgments Act 1982 (c. 27) [U.K.].

[6] Von Mehren, 'L'apport du droit comparé à la théorie et à la pratique du droit international privé', 29 *rev.int.dr.comp.* 433 (1977) (= 26 *Am.J.Comp.L.* (Supp.) 31 (1978)).

and should lead to consistent results in different countries. Comparative law has always been central to private international law. Think of the influence of Voet and Huber from the Netherlands, of Dumoulin from France, or the American Story, whose *Commentaries on the Conflict of Laws* were praised by Savigny and frequently cited by him.[7] Savigny was also much influenced by the *Traité du droit international privé* by the Frenchman Foelix.[8] Another great figure in private international law, von Wächter, took a different line and wrote that constant reference to English and American law made it hard to present German law properly, but it was Savigny's view which won through. The draftsman of the conflicts rules in the Introductory Book to the BGB made good use of comparative law, and in more recent times one can instance the shock waves sent through German law by the American theory of 'governmental interest analysis'.

Comparative law lies at the very roots of private international law, in its basic concept, the principle of nationality. This principle is not of German origin, but comes from the Code civil (art. 3 par. 3) and the Italian Mancini. Renvoi was discovered in the *Forgo* case in France (1878–82), whence it proceeded to conquer the world. Characterization cases also involve constant recourse to comparative law in order to ascertain which area of substantive law is the right one, a problem which can also arise in municipal law, for example, in deciding whether the liability of the state is a matter of private or of public law.[9] One issue where the problem arises in private international law is that of 'piercing the corporate veil' (*Haftungsdurchgriff*): is this a question of company law, calling for the application of the law of the company, or a matter of contract law, calling for the *lex contractus*, or of tort and the *lex delicti*?

[7] Savigny, 8 *System des heutigen römischen Rechts* vi, (1849; repr. Bad Homburg, 1961); Gale, 'A Very German Legal Science: Savigny and the Historical School', 17 *Stan.J.Int'l L.* 123 (1982); Nadelmann, 'Bicentennial Observations on the Second Edition of Joseph Story's *Commentaries on the Conflict of Laws*', 28 *Am.J.Comp.L.* 67 (1980).

[8] (2nd edn., Paris, 1847).

[9] BVerfGE 61, 149.

It was in relation to this problem of characterization that Rabel developed his comparative law method and thereby 'emancipated' thinking in private international law, in what Zweigert calls a 'third school' of private international law. Rabel may not have had many followers, but he certainly made people more aware of the importance of comparative law when the *lex fori* is faced with a question of characterization. This is apparent from the formula regularly used by the Bundesgerichtshof in characterization cases:

> One must ascertain the sense and purpose of the provisions of the foreign law in the light of the place they occupy in that foreign law, and then compare them with the institutions of German law. They are then to be fitted into the categories of the German conflict rules which themselves are based on the concepts and classifications of our own legal system.[10]

It is a question whether the judge in Germany should apply private international law ex officio or only at the request of a party. This is called the question of 'facultative conflicts law',[11] and again we need to take comparative law into account. Influences from France, England, and the United States are discernible.[12] And it goes without saying that comparative law is required when general principles of law are to be applied as supplemental law (*Ersatzrecht*).[13]

Some of the basic tools of the law of international contracts have been provided by comparative law, such as the German doctrine of the 'centre of gravity' of the contractual relationship, and the principle of 'characteristic performance' contained in the EEC Convention on the Law Applicable to Contractual Obligations,[14] which was laid down by the Swiss

[10] BGH, IPRspr. 1966–67, no. 19.

[11] Flessner, 'Fakultative Kollisionsrecht', 34 *RabelsZ* 547 (1970).

[12] Thomas, 'Proof of Foreign Law in Texas', 25 *Sw.L.J.* 554 (1971); *Hurtado* v. *Superior Court of Sacramento County*, 552 P.2d 666, 670 (Cal. 1974).

[13] Kötz, 'Allgemeine Rechtsgrundsätze als Ersatzrecht', 34 *RabelsZ* 663 (1970); BGHZ 69, 387; BGH, IPRax 1983, 193.

[14] Art. 4 par. 2. See Cheshire & North, *Private International Law* 504–6 (11th edn., London, 1987).

Bundesgericht,[15] and followed by the Bundesgerichtshof as to the law applicable in cases of set-off.[16]

One may briefly recall the 'loosening of the lex delicti',[17] the application of the *lex delicti* to the victim's direct claim against a liability insurer,[18] and the usefulness of comparative law in the application of Art. 6 of the Introductory Law to the BGB (*ordre public*).[19] The legal values involved here are not purely national, and comparative law can give the required international dimension by showing whether a particular rule is 'deviant' or 'a phenomenon frequently found in foreign systems'.[20]

Comparative law is of particular importance for international company law. Here we have the familiar conflict between the incorporation theory and the seat or domicile theory, which has recently gained ground in German law.[21] Both theories came to us from abroad, the seat theory from Belgium and France, the incorporation theory from England. Partisans of both views enlist the support of comparative law—and sometimes blame their opponents for not doing it properly. Grasmann and Sandrock both draw on American experience for their pseudo-foreign corporation approaches, a 'product of California' and the Berkeley Law School.[22] Proponents of the theory of domicile repay in kind and point to the catastrophic results of the incorporation theory in the United States. Discussion of the law relating to joint ventures is equally permeated by comparative law:[23] the theory of control originated in England.[24]

[15] BGE 79 II 295. [16] BGHZ 38, 254, 258, and BGE 77 II 189.

[17] Kropholler, 'Ein Anknüpfungssystem für das Deliktsstatut', 33 *RabelsZ* 601 (1969).

[18] BGH, IPRspr. 1973, 17. [19] BGHZ 22, 162; 35, 324, 331.

[20] Kropholler, 'Die vergleichende Methode und das internationale Privatrecht', 77 *ZVglRW* 1 (1978); BGHZ 54, 132.

[21] See now *R.* v. *H.M. Treasury & Customs & Excise, ex p. Daily Mail & General Trust*, (E.C.J. case 81/87) [1988] 3 C.M.L.R. 713.

[22] Grasmann, *System des internationalen Gesellschaftsrechts* (1970); Sandrock, 'Die multinationalen Korporationen im Internationalen Privatrecht', in 18 *Bericht der Deutschen Gesellschaft für Völkerrecht* 169 (1978).

[23] *Diamond Mining & Management Inc.* v. *Globe Materials Inc.*, 421 F.Supp. 70 (N.D.Cal. 1976).

[24] *Daimler Company Ltd.* v. *Continental Tyre & Rubber Co.* [1916] 2 A.C. 307.

Private international law does not only make use of comparative law; it sometimes does the comparisons itself, as when it has to decide whether one rule is 'similar' or 'more favourable', 'equally good' or 'better' than another.

5

International Business Law

As regards international business law, which is perhaps turning into world business law, the situation is similar. Here comparative law gives us not only many of the details but the concept itself. The very novelty of the questions involved often demands a comparative survey.

First there is the 'genuine link' theory, stemming from the decision of the International Court of Justice in the *Nottebohm* case,[1] which has been worked out in many fields. One of these is the 'effects theory', originating in the United States[2] and now rightly being challenged, mainly in the light of American experience. Comparative law is needed for a full appreciation of its finer details, as Rehbinder shows.[3] As we have seen, England gave us the increasingly important control theory. The list could easily be continued: the application of foreign public law,[4] the efforts to limit international jurisdiction under §23 of the Code of Civil Procedure, the doctrine of *forum non conveniens*, the dangers of forum-shopping,[5] and the 'blocking-statutes' designed to prevent abuse of discovery procedures.[6]

Many legal questions owe their vitality to comparative law simply because no one country can supply sufficient material for study; comparative law allows one to anticipate the case which has not yet arisen. This applies to the international

[1] The *Nottebohm* case, [1955] I.C.J.Rep. 4.

[2] *United States* v. *Aluminum Corp.*, 148 F.2d 416 (2d Cir. 1945).

[3] Immenga & Mestmäcker, *GWB* (Munich, 1981), Commentary to §98 par. 2 (Rehbinder).

[4] Lipstein, 'Conflict of Laws and Public Law', in Banakas (ed.), *United Kingdom Law in the 1980s* 38 (London, 1988); Forsyth, 'The Role of Public Law in the English Conflict of Laws', ibid. at 94.

[5] Baade, 'An Overview of Transnational Parallel Litigation: Recommended Strategies', 1 *Rev. of Litigation* 191 (1981).

[6] Grossfeld & Rogers, 'A Shared Values Approach to Jurisdictional Conflicts in International Economic Law', 32 *I.C.L.Q.* 931 (1983).

law of restraints on competition and protection of investors, as well as to the problem of obtaining evidence abroad and the treatment of foreign laws regarding privileged and confidential information.[7] We would be trying to think in a vacuum were it not for the way preliminary studies in comparative law can augment the material to be studied and make it easier to identify the problems.

[7] Grossfeld, *Internationales Unternehmensrecht* 232 (Heidelberg, 1986).

6

Domestic Law

I. PRELIMINARY

The preceding sections on private international law and international economic law were relatively easy. Now we must approach the hard centre: what use is comparative law to domestic law?

The contribution is most obvious where the law results from international unification, such as the law of negotiable instruments and cheques[1]—and the same is true now that the law of accounting is harmonized in Europe—but Aubin also adduces evidence for constitutional law.[2]

This sudden modulation to constitutional law may come as something of a surprise, but in fact it is public law which provides me with the perfect example. It is not too much to say that modern German administrative law begins in 1886 with a famous book by Otto Mayer,[3] the recognized 'founder and classical exponent of the methods of modern administrative law in Germany'. Mayer's work was said by Forsthoff to owe 'more to the structure of French administrative law than to any administrative practice in Germany'.[4] English models figure in the work of von Gneist, who made English ideas of self-government bear fruit in our communal autonomy. We may note in passing that the division of power between Bürgermeister and town clerk in the erstwhile British Zone is English in origin. Domestic tax law also, as Klaus Vogel has recently reminded us, is open

[1] Cairns, 'Comparative Law, Unification and Scholarly Creation of a New Ius Commune', 32 *N.I.L.Q.* 272.

[2] Aubin, 'Die rechtsvergleichende Konkretisierung von Kontrollmassstäben des Verfassungsrechts und des Kollisionsrechts in der deutschen Rechtsprechung', in *Deutsche Landesreferate zum VII. Internationalen Kongress für Rechtsvergleichung in Uppsala 1966* 99 (Tübingen, 1967).

[3] *Theorie des französischen Verwaltungsrechts* (Strasburg, 1866).

[4] Forsthoff, 1 *Lehrbuch des Verwaltungsrechts* 51 (10th edn., Munich, 1973).

to comparative law, for example as regards the impact of principles of commercial law on accounting for tax purposes (the principle of *Massgeblichkeit* as laid down in §5 of the Income Tax Act).

2. PRIVATE LAW

This may not impress the dyed-in-the-wool privatist, who is probably muttering that he wants hard evidence. So we must face the music: 'what contribution does comparative law make to the study of private law?'

Let us start with what is apparently the most 'German' part, with the theory of contract and the concept of the *Anspruch* or 'claim'. As to the concept of 'claim', Windscheid went to France for it. As to contract, comparative law has illuminated for us the way it actually operates in our legal and economic system, particularly by letting us see how the idea of contract gets on in a planned economy.[5]

The effects of comparative law reach the very heartland of doctrine. As is well known, the doctrine of the will is on the wane and the idea of reliance is coming to the fore. Comparative law did not initiate the movement, but it added speed and momentum. We learnt from the English doctrine of consideration how contract law can emerge from tort, and how, by building on the notion of quid pro quo and reliance, one can have a system of contract law without having any theory of the will at all.

The connections between consideration and contract theory have been demonstrated quite recently by Köndgen,[6] though in his treatment of reliance as functionally contractual he perhaps goes too far, under Californian influence, in dismantling the theory of consensus. The United States offers such a range of methods[7] that we should not be too ready

[5] Grossfeld, 'Money Sanctions for Breach of Contract in a Communist Economy', 72 *Yale L.J.* 1326 (1963); Hazard, 'Pourquoi le droit comparé? L'URSS et les États-Unis', 56 *rev.dr.int.dr.comp.* 292 (1979).

[6] Köndgen, *Selbstbindung ohne Vertrag* (Tübingen, 1981).

[7] Gilmore, *The Ages of American Law* (New Haven, 1977).

to embrace any one of them or to undermine the legal institutions with which we are familiar. Our need for legal doctrine is greater than theirs, if only because it offers an economical means of dealing with constantly recurring problems.[8]

We also have comparative law to thank for opening our eyes to the problems of exemption clauses and general conditions of business. Ludwig Raiser's famous work on exemption clauses is very heavily based on comparative law in its doctrinal sections;[9] indeed Ferid refers to it as a 'masterpiece of comparative law'.[10] Comparative law also helps where novel phenomena such as the 'letter of intent' have to be integrated into existing doctrine.

The same is true in the law of damages. The estoppel doctrine of English and American law was one model for our law of *Verwirkung*, and traces of comparative law can be found in causation theory and in the rules of mistake in sales contracts. So in tort law. Comparative law has emphasized the context in which tort law operates, and has helped to overcome the sterile notion that compensation is its sole purpose and concern.[11] Relevant slogans here are fault liability/strict liability, deterrence, social costs, and economic analysis of law. Works by Tunc[12] and von Hippel[13] have brought home to us the close relationship between tort and insurance.

But in matters of detail the influence goes deeper. Think of the notion of duties of care (*Verkehrspflichten*) and the

[8] Grossfeld, *Zivilrecht als Gestaltungsaufgabe* 86 (Heidelberg, 1977).

[9] Raiser, *Das Recht der Allgemeinen Geschäftsbedingungen* (Bad Homburg, 1935).

[10] Ferid, 'Die derzeitige Lage von Rechtsvergleichung und IPR in der Bundesrepublik Deutschland', 22 *ZfRV* 86 (1981).

[11] 'Compensation' is the fourth of the eighteen 'Purposes and Policy Goals of Tort Law' identified by Marshall Shapo, the Reporter of *Towards a Jurisprudence of Injury: The Continuing Creation of a System of Substantive Justice in American Tort Law* (Report to American Bar Association, 1984). See also Grossfeld, 'Haftpflichtversicherung im Wandel', *Versicherungswirtschaft* 693 (1974).

[12] Tunc, *La Securité routière* (Paris, 1966).

[13] Von Hippel, *Schadensausgleich bei Verkehrsunfällen—Haftungsersetzung durch Versicherungsschutz* (Berlin, 1968); see also Fleming, Hellner, & von Hippel, *Haftungsersetzung durch Versicherungsschutz* (Frankfurt, 1980).

probing works of von Caemmerer, Deutsch, and von Bar.[14] In products liability we have the pioneering work of Werner Lorenz[15] and the pervasive influence of American law. The same is true of the general right of personality, with leading roles being played by the Swiss model and the American law of privacy.[16] When the Bundesgerichtshof first decided that damages might be awarded for non-economic harm it cited no foreign precedent,[17] but comparative law was deployed later in its defence of its decision,[18] and foreign examples were used by the Federal Constitutional Court when it upheld the Bundesgerichtshof.[19] The notion of *solatium* or *Genugtuung* under §847 BGB in cases of infringement of the general right of personality comes directly from Swiss law.[20] Comparative law has also played a role in the question whether the birth of a child can be regarded as 'harm'.[21]

As to commercial law 'leasing', 'factoring', 'travellers-cheques', and 'credit-cards' are all words which come from abroad, and as anyone familiar with the significance of language for law will realize—a matter to which we shall return—legal ideas come with the words.

3. BUSINESS ASSOCIATIONS

A mere glance at the law of business associations shows that important theoretical questions are much affected by comparative law. The French *société de fait* led us to the

[14] Von Caemmerer, 'Wandlungen des Deliktsrechts', in 2 *Hundert Jahre Deutsches Rechtsleben, Festschrift zum hundertjährigen Bestehen des deutschen Juristentages 1860–1960* 49; Deutsch, 1 *Haftungsrecht* (*Allgemeine Lehren*) (Cologne, 1976); von Bar, *Verkehrspflichten: Richterliche Gefahrsteuerungsgebote im deutschen Deliktsrecht* (Cologne, 1980).

[15] Lorenz, *Die Haftung des Warenherstellers, Arbeiten zur Rechtsvergleichung* (Karlsruhe, 1962); von Caemmerer, 'Products Liability', 2 *Festschrift Rheinstein* 659 (Tübingen, 1969).

[16] Warren & Brandeis, 'The Right to Privacy', 4 *Harv.L.Rev.* 193 (1891).

[17] BGHZ 26, 349.

[18] BGHZ 39, 124, 132.

[19] BVerfGE 34, 269, 289, 291.

[20] BGHZ 18, 149, 155.

[21] BGH NJW 1983, 1371, 1373.

idea of the de facto corporation, reminded us of the problems posed by an 'immortal' economic unit, and showed us the error of anthropomorphism in relation to legal persons. Serick, Drobnig, Müller-Freienfels, and Rehbinder[22] have shown us through comparative law that the problem of 'piercing the veil' of legal persons is a general one, though we may perhaps have been beguiled by American impatience with legal forms and assumed too hastily that the internal structure of legal personality was the same in the two systems. So, too, with the reverse claim, when a shareholder's creditor seeks to reach corporate assets. The tension between the formality of minimum capital requirements and the realities of corporate financing has also come in for debate. Comparative law did useful preliminary work in preparing the ground for discussion of the shareholder's action in Germany. Although there is no reference to comparative law in the opinion in which the Bundesgerichtshof accepted that an individual shareholder whose legal rights have been seriously infringed may bring an action against the company,[23] this is doubtless on the good old principle that 'the Moor has done his duty: he may go'.

As to the problem of insider-trading in securities law, our eyes were first opened by American law.[24] Comparative law will have an increased role to play in the law of accounting after the Fourth and Seventh EEC Directives. For example, its central notion of 'a picture which reflects the actual facts' (§237 par. 2 sec. 2 Commercial Code) comes from the English 'true and fair view', and is incomprehensible without reference to it; the notion of 'good will' betrays similar influences. The

[22] Serick, *Rechtsreform und Realität juristischer Personen* (Berlin, 1955); Drobnig, *Haftungsdurchgriff bei Kapitalgesellschaften* (Frankfurt, 1959); Müller-Freienfels, 'Zur Lehre vom Durchgriff bei juristischen Personen', 156 *ACP* 522 (1957); Rehbinder, *Konzernaussenrecht und allgemeines Privatrecht* (Bad Homburg, 1969).

[23] BGH JZ 1982, 602; Grossfeld & Brondics, 'Die Aktionärsklage—nun auch im deutschen Recht', *JZ* 1982, 589; Buxbaum, 'Extension of Parent Company Shareholders' Rights to Participate in the Governance of Subsidiaries', 31 *Am.J.Comp.L.* 11 (1983).

[24] Tunc, 'A French Lawyer Looks at American Corporation Law and Securities Regulation', 130 *U.Pa.L.Rev.* 757 (1982).

valuation of a business by means of the discounted earnings method also shows foreign influence. The same is true of the liability of the accountant and for the technique of the 'world-wide balance-sheet'. As to the law of businesses, I note in passing that the very notion of *Konzern*, the relations between parent and subsidiary, came to us from England through Austria, and remind one of the lasting impact of Mestmäcker's comparative study.[25]

4. ANTI-TRUST LAW

Writers on anti-trust law think it almost a professional duty to invoke the law of the United States, yet I sometimes wonder whether the American view of competition, affected as it is by culture and geography, is quite so relevant to the very different, less mercurial and strident conditions over here. At any rate comparability should not be assumed, as it tends to be today; it must be established in each case. It gives one pause for thought to glance at a local newspaper in the United States with its frenzy of depreciatory comparative advertising, or to take an evening drive through the glitter and storm of advertising in Dallas or Los Angeles or Las Vegas, with all the 'discounts', 'special rates', 'special sales', and myriad other ways of indicating prices.

These examples of the contribution made by comparative law must suffice. The reader can undoubtedly produce other examples from his own specialty.

[25] Mestmäcker, *Verwaltung, Konzerngewalt und Rechte der Aktionäre* (Karlsruhe, 1958); Heemann, 'L'influence du droit comparé sur le projet belge de réforme des sociétés commerciales', 2 *Festschrift Coing* 125 (Munich, 1982).

7

Law in the Courts

I. SOME EXAMPLES

Let us now turn to the application of law, to the practice of the courts. Comparative law has long been said to be of use in this context, so one might think it easy to show that in fact it is often put to use; after all, 'juger, c'est comparer', as Proust observed. But great expectations are apt to be disappointed. Apart from private international law, where the Bundesgerichtshof deploys comparative law in ten per cent of the cases, the total number of judgements in private law which allude to comparative law is rather slight.

Some examples have already been given in the discussion of legal theory. We can add decisions of the Bundesgerichtshof on water law,[1] and especially one on §89 b of the Commercial Code, which cites Italian, Swiss, and Austrian sources.[2] Further references can be found in Dölle[3] and Aubin.[4] It should also be borne in mind that the Federal Constitutional Court 'is quite open-minded and receptive to comparative law'.[5]

In general comparative law is used to reinforce decisions already arrived at, as a subsidiary method of interpretation. Comparisons are made within 'the circle of systems culturally linked by common ethical standards':[6] German-speaking

[1] BGHZ 30, 382.

[2] BGHZ 24, 214, 218f.

[3] Dölle, 'Der Beitrag der Rechtsvergleichung zum deutschen Recht', in 2 *Hundert Jahre Deutsches Rechtsleben, Festschrift zum hundertjährigen Bestehen des Deutschen Juristentages 1860–1960* 33 (Karlsruhe, 1960).

[4] Aubin, 'Die rechtsvergleichende Konkretisierung von Kontrollmassstäben des Verfassungsrechts und des Kollisionsrechts in der deutschen Rechtsprechung', in *Deutsche Landesreferate zum VII. Internationalen Kongress für Rechtsvergleichung in Uppsala 1966* 99 (Tübingen, 1976).

[5] Aubin, 'Die rechtsvergleichende Interpretation autonominternen Rechts in der deutschen Rechtsprechung', 34 *RabelsZ* 458 (1970).

[6] Aubin (above n. 4).

neighbours are in the forefront, first Switzerland and then Austria, with French and English law making occasional appearances. Sometimes the Bundesgerichtshof considers and expressly rejects an argument drawn from comparative law, as in one case concerning Austrian law.[7]

2. SOME PROBLEMS

But we must not be misled by the fact that direct references to foreign law are fairly sparse. Comparative law is more important than the figures suggest, for it works its way into judicial decision-making through the medium of the literature and theory which it informs. This saves the courts from doing their own comparative law, although it makes it harder to establish the impact of comparative law in any particular case. Maybe the decision was affected by comparative law without mentioning it, maybe it would have been just the same without it—the time may simply have been ripe. The famous 'chicken-pest' case is a good example:[8] though the expression 'strict liability' was used,[9] the Bundesgerichtshof did not allude to any foreign precedents, yet foreign solutions figured so largely in the literature cited by the court that one can hardly suppose it took no account of them.

Of course comparatists may occasionally lay claim to an idea which reached us and altered our ways of thinking without any of their doing. Media coverage of a demonstration in Berkeley or Amsterdam or Zurich may have a greater impact than anything we may later do, and often we do it much later. But such doubts attach to all forms of legal activity, not just comparative law; indeed they attach to the efficacy of the law itself.[10] What effect do we really have? How different would the world be if we didn't do our job? A large question!

[7] BGH, NJW 1981, 1206.

[8] BGHZ 51, 91; in English in Markesinis, *The German Law of Torts: A Comparative Introduction* 245–56 (Oxford, 1986).

[9] BGHZ 51, 91, 98.

[10] Allott, *The Limits of Law* (London, 1980).

To return to the relationship between judicial decision and writings on comparative law, there are those who blame the courts for not having 'the world-citizen's attitude towards foreign law'. I do not agree with them. Given the difficulty of doing serious comparative law and the limited resources they have available for it, the courts are wise to be tentative. Comparative law, as I observed earlier, is chiefly a matter for scholars and writers.

8

Constraints

Has comparative law ever failed? you may ask. Well, you may ask but you cannot expect me to give the game away. I just hope that you have been as impressed as I am by these examples of the effect of comparative law, or rather, of the influence of foreign laws, even though no mention has been made of Roman Law, Canon Law, the Law of Lombardy or the Netherlands or the Code Napoléon. But this is perhaps not so surprising when one considers the geography and history of Germany: we are part of a common European tradition which even in the era of nation-states retained much of its strength.

I. MECHANISMS OF INFLUENCE

How does foreign law come to exercise such an influence? We cannot fully explain the causes or the means, but the outcome squares with Watson's observation that the native element in the law of any country is relatively slight:[1] 'Law develops mainly by borrowing', he says.[2] Legal systems have always been subject to supranational forces, often to a predominant extent.[3] It is far from clear why or how such interchange takes place. We speak vaguely of this complex and common phenomenon as 'the infiltration of legal ideas',[4] but those who have tried to ascertain the reasons for this peculiar osmosis usually end up describing rather than explaining it.[5] The principle of economy which runs through

[1] Watson, *The Making of the Civil Law* 181 (Cambridge, Mass., 1981).

[2] Ibid. 183.

[3] Ibid. 186, 187.

[4] Ibid. 53, 181; Gaudemet, 'Les transferts de droit', 27 *L'Année sociologique* 29 (1976).

[5] Watson (above n. 1) 182; Watson, 'Comparative Law and Legal Change', 37 *Camb.L.J.* 319, 321 (1978).

all European thinking is certainly part of it. One thing is clear in any case: the process cannot be explained in purely rational or functional terms.[6] Certainly the role played by professional comparatists is by no means a leading one. Powerful irrational forces, as yet unrevealed, are at work; probe as we will, law remains a mystery.

2. MAINTAINING CULTURAL IDENTITY

We need not fall victim to 'international euphoria' just because we recognize the extent to which our legal culture has been permeated and affected by foreign elements. Indeed, we are answerable for the continuing identity of the great legal tradition we represent. Comparative law does not mean simply absorbing foreign law. It often serves to bar the entry of foreign legal ideas, to confirm the traditional institutions of law and to enhance the respect they merit. Examples from my own specialties are the debate over 'governmental interest analysis', the confirmation of the theory of domicile in international company law, and the preservation of our system of running companies by means of a board of management and a supervisory board with votes cast by depositees rather than by means of a board of directors and proxy-voting.[7] We must have constant regard for our own culture while remaining amenable to foreign influence. Hence the tasks and limits of comparative law. There is a further reason for not making too much of comparative law: our knowledge is limited, for complete understanding of a foreign legal institution is almost impossible to attain. Our vision is culturally blinkered, our expertise often built on sand.

[6] Beckström, 'Transplantation of Legal Systems: An Early Report on the Reception of Western Law in Ethiopia', 21 *Am.J.Comp.L.* 557 (1973); Beckström, 'Handicaps of Legal-Social Engineering in a Developing Nation', 22 *Am.J.Comp.L.* 697 (1974).

[7] Grossfeld, 'Management and Control of Marketable Share Companies', in 13 *Int.Enc.Comp.Law* ch. 4; Grossfeld & Ebke, 'Controlling the Modern Corporation: A Comparative View of Corporate Power in the United States and Europe', 26 *Am.J.Comp.L.* 397 (1978).

3. DIFFICULTIES

The time has come to speak of the 'weakness' of comparative law, its inherent difficulties. What limits are there to the contribution which comparative law can make to our law? It is not really a problem of the particular subject-matter, for comparative law reaches into almost all areas of private law, into family law (equal rights of the spouses,[8] principle of the breakdown of the marriage, family courts) and the law of succession (the rights of illegitimate children). No area of law is a priori resistant to comparative law.

But comparative law is necessarily superficial. If we can hardly grasp our own legal system as a functioning whole, how can we grasp a foreign one? Let us admit this superficiality, and not boast of the 'eagle-eye of the comparatist'. Comparative law is unsystematic, incomplete, a thing of shreds and patches. Then there is the question of suitability for comparison. Which legal institutions in which legal systems can we compare? How akin must the systems be in culture or civilization?[9] It is not easy to find exact counterparts in different systems, to decide whether an institution is transferable or what adaptation is possible.[10] This problem was not too acute as long as comparative law was mainly concerned with Western European cultures, but when we look to the United States the matter is already less easy, as we shall see, and it becomes really difficult when we look to Africa and Asia.

4. DANGERS

Comparative law is a powerful weapon, but also a dangerous one. As Koschaker said, 'Bad comparative law is worse than

[8] BGHZ 11, Supp., 34, 61.

[9] Kamba, 'Comparative Law: A Theoretical Framework', 23 *I.C.L.Q.* 485, 506 (1974).

[10] Watson, *Legal Transplants: An Approach to Comparative Law* 8 (Edinburgh, 1974).

none at all.'[11] Not only must one always be conscious of its limitations, but it must always go hand in hand with work on domestic law. It must never become the preserve of specialists in foreign law but remain in the hands of those who are responsible for domestic legal culture at home. The point is well made by the Spanish-South American poet Juan Ramón Jiménez. These words of his are inscribed on a fountain on the campus of the University of Puerto Rico in San Juan: 'Pie en la patria casual o eligida; corazon, cabeza en el aire del mundo', or 'Keep your feet on your native or chosen homeland and your head and heart in the air of the world'.

[11] Cited by van Dunné, 'The Use of Comparative Law by the Legislator in the Netherlands', *Netherlands Reports to the Eleventh International Congress on Comparative Law* 37 (1983).

9

Culture and Law

1. THE UNIQUENESS OF LEGAL SYSTEMS

These limitations on comparative law arise from the fact that every legal system is a 'unique product of a particular complex of determining factors':[1] 'Every culture has its particular law, and every law its particular cultural life.'[2] Every legal system has a unique individuality. This is entailed in the saying that 'law varies directly with culture'.[3] Law is culture and culture is law. The idea that the law of a culture stems from the material and spiritual life of the people is as old as law itself: phrases such as 'common sense' (from *sensus communis*), 'vox populi, vox dei', and 'Volksgeist' are there to show it. But no culture is an island, every culture gives and receives, and the resulting mixtures may obscure differences; so we must be more than usually perceptive and discriminating.

2. SOCIETY AND LAW

Even our initial position, that law, culture, and society are indissolubly linked, has not gone unchallenged. Alan Watson, a Scot now in the United States, is one of the challengers. He objects that 'in many cases legal rules are equally at home in many places',[4] and proposes[5] to show that law and society

[1] Constantinesco, 'Die Kulturkreise als Grundlage der Rechtskreise', *ZfRV* 161, 174 (1981). I am indebted to Professor William Bridge of the Southern Methodist University School of Law for his stimulating collaboration in this section.

[2] Kohler, *Das Recht als Kulturerscheinung* 5 (Würzburg, 1885); Glendon, Gordon, & Osakwe, *Comparative Legal Traditions* (St Paul, 1982). Wilhelm Arnold put it well: 'Only when the "jurist" has learnt to feel the bonds and constraints imposed by all that makes him a member of his time and society does he first become really free and able to overcome these constraints'; Arnold, *Cultur und Rechtsleben* vii (Berlin, 1865).

[3] Donald Black, *The Behavior of Law* 63 (New York, 1976).

[4] Watson, *Society and Legal Change* 130 (Edinburgh, 1977).

[5] Watson, 'Legal Transplants and Law Reform', 92 *Law Q.Rev.* 79, 81 n. 12 (1976).

are not necessarily connected:[6] 'Whatever their historical origins may have been, rules of private law can survive without any close connection to any particular people, any particular period of time or any particular place.'[7]

Watson points to the way Roman Law survived under entirely altered circumstances, he reminds us that the civil law tradition is common to countries as different as Germany and Paraguay, and shows how German and French law were received in Japan and elsewhere. Then, too, legal rules are often unresponsive to the needs of the society in question,[8] law is often dysfunctional, at any rate in Western systems.[9] There is good evidence for this in the way we moan about the quantity of legislation: law is not felt to answer our needs, even though we make it ourselves.

For Watson law and society diverge not because the legal rules were originally inappropriate[10] but because they outlast changes in society: this power of survival 'is one of the most striking features of legal rules'. 'Legal rules, once created, live on,' as he puts it.[11] They are beyond the experience and understanding of laymen, and survive because most people are indifferent and the jurists have a stake in their doctrinal niceties.[12] Traditionalism in law and culture is the strongest force.[13] Pascal puts the point very dramatically: 'By the pure light of reason, nothing is just *per se*: it all depends on time. What is just is determined by custom, simply by dint of being accepted as such; this is the mystical basis of its authority, and if you trace it back to its origin you destroy it.'[14]

[6] Watson, *The Nature of Law* 95 (Edinburgh, 1977).
[7] Watson (above n. 5).
[8] Watson (above n. 4) 5, 130.
[9] Watson, *The Making of the Civil Law* 187 (Cambridge, Mass., 1981).
[10] Bohannan, 9 *International Encyclopedia of Social Sciences* 76 (London, 1968).
[11] Watson (above n. 4) 8; see also Epstein, 'The Social Consequences of Common Law Rules', 95 *Harv.L.Rev.* 1717 (1982); Epstein, 'The Static Conception of the Common Law', 9 *J.Leg.Stud.* 253 (1980); Williams, 'The Static Conception of the Common Law: A Comment', 9 *J.Leg.Stud.* 277 (1980).
[12] Watson (above n. 4) 8, 115.
[13] Ibid. 186, 187.
[14] Pascal, *Pensées* no. 230, p. 81 (ed. Chevalier, Paris, 1937).

3. TRADITION AS A HISTORICAL FORCE[15]

Watson's purpose in emphasizing the autonomy of law, legal ideas, and legal tradition as a creative force is to prevent law becoming trivialized by sociology.[16] I am with him in his desire to stop such an erosion of legal anthropology. But we must not throw the baby out with the bath-water. Watson's black-and-white view is itself culturally determined, steeped as he is in the tenacious traditionalism of Scots and English law. We central Europeans are not blessed with so unbroken a tradition. After all, the industrial revolution and two World Wars have changed our law very greatly—one only has to think of 'product liability' and 'frustration of the transaction' to see that. It is true that there was no change in the wording of the BGB, but that is entirely irrelevant. More recently the sexual revolution has left its mark on the rules of immorality and extra-marital relationships, again without any alteration in the letter of the law.

4. TRADITION AND LAW

Yet though Watson exaggerates somewhat, there is truth in what he says. Comparatists keep coming across the same or similar legal ideas and institutions, perhaps with a different twist; the 'recurrence of legal forms' is a familiar phenomenon.[17] Every society, every legal system is a prisoner of its history; tradition has its effect even if the world around has changed. The tenaciousness of law is assisted by legal language, by legal technique, by legal education, and by the stuff of law itself, in brief by lawyer's law, as well as by the principles of inertia and economy. We need only think of the 'principle of abstraction' in our own law of property to realize what is meant. Often the best explanation of a legal

[15] Kamp & Wollasch, *Tradition als historische Kraft* (Berlin, 1982); compare 'It is from the folly not the wisdom of our ancestors that we have so much to learn', Bentham, cited by Hart, *Essays on Bentham* 9 (Oxford, 1982).

[16] Watson (above n. 9) 183.

[17] Mayer-Maly, 'Die Wiederkehr der Rechtsfiguren', *JZ* 1971, 1.

institution lies in its history rather than in its current operation. And the efficacy of law is something we are learning very clearly in the Common Market: law is the motor of the European Communities.

One can see the tenacity of law as either negative or positive, independently of one's position as progressive or conservative. Goethe has Mephistopheles, no less, present the negative view:

> Laws are transmitted, like some dread disease,
> Father to son, and spread from place to place.
> Reason turns folly, boon becomes a bane
> To later generations. Yet the law
> Innate in us is meanwhile quite ignored.[18]

On the positive side, tradition helps to preserve cultural identity, to temper the excesses of the latest fashion, to curb the most powerful interests of the day, and to maintain continuity and stability. Tradition is a democracy where predecessors have a vote. To this extent law is an expression of cultural experience, of an understanding exceeding that of a single generation. This less obvious function is a valuable one, and the special stability we deliberately attach to constitutional law shows that we actually do value it.[19]

5. THE CONSEQUENCES FOR COMPARATIVE LAW

The implications are obvious. Neither the functional/sociological approach nor the approach based on history or the history of ideas is by itself adequate for comparative law: both approaches must be borne in mind. This might produce an overwhelming profusion and variety of data, were it not for a fact already mentioned, that the same or similar basic themes, albeit with variations, keep cropping up in

[18] Goethe, *Faust*, Part One, The Student Scene. Compare Jefferson's view that 'There should be a revolution every twenty years': Wills, *Inventing America, Jefferson's Declaration of Independence* 124 (New York, 1978).

[19] e.g. Art. 79 par. 2, 3, Basic Law.

comparative law and legal history.[20] Nevertheless the range of contributory factors does make it very difficult to make sense of any legal system, even in part.[21] Research on our present topic, the Reception, has taught us as much.[22] For this purpose it is essential for us to understand the social, political and cultural background of the foreign law and comprehend the organic nature of its rules.

6. 'IDEAS' AND THEIR SOCIAL CONTEXT

Another of Watson's views is specific to comparative law:[23] he is optimistic about the possibility of transplanting legal institutions.[24] He believes that one need not know much about the social background in either the donor or the recipient system: one just has to find an 'idea' capable of importation.[25]

With this I cannot agree. Certainly foreign law can give us an 'idea', a stimulus, an intellectual spark. That is already a good deal, for ideas are in short supply and we should seize them whenever we can, even if we don't know how useful they have proved elsewhere. For example, we can learn a good deal from what American courts had to say on the distinction between procedural and substantive law in cases

[20] Mayer-Maly (above n. 17); Grossfeld, ' "Unsterblichkeit" und Jurisprudenz', *Festschrift Kummer* (Berne, 1980); Stein, 'Uses, Misuses and Nonuses of Comparative Law', 72 *Nw.U.L.Rev.* 198, 206 f. (1977); Kahn-Freund, 'Comparative Law as an Academic Subject', 82 *L.Q.Rev.* 40 (1966).

[21] McKnight, 'Some Observations on Mixed Systems of Law', 22 *Jur.Rev.* 177 (1977); Marshall, 'The Future of "Received" English Law in the Countries of the Commonwealth, 15 *Comp. & Int.L.J.S.Africa* 81 (1982); Beinart, 'The English Legal Contribution in South Africa: The Interaction of Civil Law and Common Law', *Acta Juridica* 7 (1981); Abel, 'Western Courts in Non-Western Settings: Problems of Court Use in Colonial and Neo-Colonial Africa', in Burman, Hassell, & Bond, *The Imposition of Law* 167 (New York, 1979).

[22] Kahn-Freund (above n. 20) 40; von Mehren, 'The Significance of Cultural and Legal Diversity for International Transactions', 1 *Festschrift Rheinstein* 247 (Tübingen, 1969).

[23] Watson (above n. 5).

[24] Watson, *Legal Transplants: An Approach to Comparative Law* (Edinburgh, 1974); more realistic is Holldack, *Grenzen der Erkenntnis ausländischen Rechts* 102 (Leipzig, 1919).

[25] Watson (above n. 5) 79; contra, Stein (above n. 20).

under the *Erie* doctrine,[26] perhaps because the question arose in a novel manner and in a remarkable context.[27] This can be of use in international company law, on the important question whether rules as to costs in shareholder suits are part of substantive or procedural law.[28] A legal idea has value in itself: it gives us a new coign of vantage, lets our imagination strike out on new paths.

But in general we must familiarize ourselves with the cultural background before we can even understand the foreign text, for the choice and meaning of the words in the text depend on its cultural background.[29] This is especially true when we adduce a foreign idea in support of a position on a point of domestic law. The persuasive force of a legal idea depends greatly on its function, context, and utility. There is always a risk of taking 'dead law' for 'living law' in a foreign system, of being misled by 'pretty words'. Distance may lend enchantment: but close inspection is what is required.

Much the same is true when the question is whether a particular idea will be of use to us. The only way to decide on the probable success of importing a foreign idea, once we have understood it, is to find out how the foreigners have fared with it. The difficulty here is that their experience took place in a natural and cultural context quite different from our own. On the other hand, a sense of this distance may help us appraise ideas which are vaunted as especially suitable. These points are all the more important when an entire legal institution rather than an isolated idea is in issue. Then it is not enough just to ascertain the rules in the foreign system, we have to find out how this system operates in actual practice, and evaluate the probable results of a transplant.

[26] The doctrine that federal courts must apply the substantive law, including conflicts law, of the state where it is sitting. *Erie R.R. Co.* v. *Tompkins* 304 U.S. 64 (1938); *Klaxon Co.* v. *Stentor Elec. Mfg. Co.* 313 U.S. 487 (1941); *Day & Zimmerman, Inc.* v. *Challoner* 423 U.S. 3 (1975).

[27] Wright, *Handbook of the Law of Federal Courts* §59, p. 271 (3rd edn., St Paul, 1976).

[28] *Cohen* v. *Beneficial Loan Co.*, 337 U.S. 541 (1948).

[29] Lon Fuller, *Anatomy of the Law* 57 (New York, 1968).

To import anything without such evaluation is, as Montesquieu said, 'un grand hasard'.

7. LAW AS CAMOUFLAGE

As soon as we leave the European legal family, a whole Pandora's box of problems opens up. Here the comparative lawyer is a mere dilettante, perhaps with all the dilettante's daring. Law and legal argument call for a *Weltanschauung* which is sympathetic as well as intellectual.[30] This is difficult enough when the law is our own, enormously more difficult when it is foreign. One major difficulty is with what is 'self-evident' in a legal system, with what goes without saying, let alone writing. We run into taboos, conspiracies of silence about underlying motivations. Language can conceal the real problem. Germans will recall the *Dictionary of Inhumanity*[31] with its appalling euphemisms such as 'final solution' and 'special treatment'; even today we speak of 'termination of pregnancy' rather than 'abortion'. The United States Constitution provides an example from abroad: in provisions now repealed slavery was called 'the peculiar institution' and the word 'slave' was sedulously avoided, but everyone knew what was meant.[32]

Legal rules, as we keep discovering, do not always reflect reality, indeed sometimes seem designed to conceal it ('window-dressing'). Think of the divorces by consent which were granted under the guise of the fault principle when divorce by consent was unobtainable,[33] or of the fiction that

[30] Brandeis, 'The Living Law', 10 *Ill.L.Rev.* 461, 470 (1915–16).

[31] Compare Sternberger & Storz, *Aus dem Wörterbuch des Unmenschen* (3rd edn., Hamburg, 1968).

[32] See Fernbacher, *The Dred Scott Case* 23, 25, 27 (New York, 1978); Stampp, *The Peculiar Institution: Slavery in the Ante-bellum South* (New York, 1956).

[33] Justice Bonynge gave a realistic appraisal of this in *Reed* v. *Littleton*, 289 N.Y.S. 798 (Sup.Ct. 1936).

Furthermore, has not my good brother overlooked the fact that a certain amount of naiveté is an essential adjunct to the judicial office? Does not the Supreme Court grind out thousands of divorces annually upon the stereotyped sin of the same big blonde attired in the same black silk pajamas? . . . Do we not daily pretend to hush up the fact that an offending defendant is insured when every juror with an ounce of wit recognizes the defendant's lawyer and his

a GmbH & Co. KG is still a personal partnership when the only general partner is a limited company,[34] or the view that interest from an investment is 'income' even though inflation has reduced the real return to zero.[35] Many of the state corporation laws in the United States are notoriously a mere façade, like social rights in the Eastern Bloc, or the English theory, apparently so liberal, of incorporation in private international law. Law can also be used quite deliberately for disseminating social and political propaganda.[36]

8. SHIFTS AS MODELS

It sometimes happens that the enactment of the measure which is really desired is impracticable, so a compromise or second-best solution is adopted. This has occurred as a result of competition between the individual states in the United States, where in the absence of federal jurisdiction the least demanding rule tends to win through. Think of corporations in Delaware, divorce in Nevada and abortion in New York. As time goes by, such rules, originally adopted under the pressure of circumstances, as a necessary evil, come to seem normal, even ideal, and are put forward for imitation abroad, their origin forgotten. Thus we often forget that investor-protection in the United States was a response to the weakness of corporation law in the several states. Only seldom can the outsider see through these veils.

entourage as old friends? More than half a century ago P. T. Barnum recorded the fact that the American people delight in being humbugged, and such is still the national mood . . .

For a generation or more betting at horse races was unlawful. After this prolonged burst of morality the Legislature suddenly discovered the need of 'improving the breed of horses' and enacted article 20 of the Membership Corporation Law . . . In a backhanded way this legislation restored racetrack betting by removing the criminal penalties. But let no one suspect that our best citizens repair to Belmont Park and other nearby tracks for the purpose of betting or gambling. Perish the thought, for their minds rest on higher things. Improving the breed of horses is their aim . . . These things a judge must believe, even at the risk of being chided as naive, because they are contemporary America.

In Germany also the jurist's life must be fiction in parts.

[34] Grossfeld, *Zivilrecht als Gestaltungsaufgabe* 42 (Heidelberg, 1977).

[35] BFH, BStBl II 1968, 143.

[36] George Orwell, 'Politics and the English Language', in Smart (ed.), *English Modern Essayists* 226 (2nd edn., New York, 1973); Weinrich, *Linguistik der Lüge* (Heidelberg, 1966).

If this is true in the narrow field in which comparative law has hitherto been practised, namely Europe, where the systems are closely related, and America, where the relationship is slightly more distant, the difficulties increase when we turn to Africa or Asia, for there even the conception of law itself may be quite different.[37]

[37] Barton, Gibbs, Li, & Merryman, *Law in Radically Different Cultures* (St Paul, 1983); Victor Li, *Law without Lawyers* (Boulder, 1978).

10

The United States Example

I. INTRODUCTION

Let me now try to show how hard it is for a comparative lawyer to reach a proper understanding of a foreign legal system.[1] It seems right to take the United States as our example because United States law is highly influential over here[2] and we often suppose that it presents no particular problems.

Yet this influence of the United States is rather surprising to anyone who has seen the great differences in geography, natural resources, and social structure, the great divergence between written law and what actually goes on.[3] Admittedly there is a great deal of interest to observe and new developments to watch; but their stage of development in state and society is so different from ours, their 'system of coordinates'[4] so dissimilar, that it may well be unnecessary or impossible for us to adopt their rules.

We see here what Watson calls a 'transplant bias': rules may often be adopted not because of their intrinsic merit, but because of their source, because of the country they come from.[5] The strength of the bias depends on linguistic similarity, the reputation and quality of the foreign legal system, the accessibility of its legal materials, and the country's politico-economic pull. Koschaker, indeed, gave this as the principal explanation of any reception: the

[1] See Atiyah, 'Lawyers and Rules: Some Anglo-American Comparisons', 37 *Sw.L.J.* 545 (1983); Atiyah & Summers, *Form and Substance in Anglo-American Law: A Comparative Study* (Oxford, 1987).

[2] Lenhoff, 'America's Legal Inventions Adopted in Other Countries', 1 *Buffalo L.Rev.* 118 (1951–2); Lenhoff, 'America's Cultural Contributions to Europe in the Realm of Law', 16 *Buffalo L.Rev.* 7 (1966–7).

[3] On the possibility of explaining trends in the EEC, see Sandalow & Stein, *Courts and Free Markets* (Oxford, 1982).

[4] Fred J. Cook, *The Crimes of Watergate* (New York, 1981).

[5] Watson, *The Making of the Civil Law* 183 (Cambridge, Mass., 1981).

authority of a country's law is related to its intellectual and cultural prestige, itself a function of the country's political power.[6]

The first difficulty facing comparative lawyers in dealing with the United States is often our failure to come to grips with the subject-matter; long familiarity causes us to be taken in by appearances. To begin with, we fail to realise how big the United States is: it is not a state at all, at any rate by our petty European standards—it is a continent! We are not dealing with unified law in a single state, as we are used to, but with the manifold diversity of a whole continent, not one but fifty Americas, or at any rate fifty states each with its own identity. America is different! Different from our picture of it. It is to demonstrate this, to show how different America is, that the following observations are made; they are not intended by way of judgement or criticism.

2. PROBLEMS OF TRANSLATION

The same words can mean different things (*faux amis*) and false conclusions may be drawn. 'Football' and 'Fussball' are utterly different games in the United States and Germany, almost classical expressions of different ways of life. Our Fussball, soccer, is a game for girls and schoolchildren over there.

Legal language can be even more deceptive. Take property taxes in the two countries. They seem to serve the same function, and so to be comparable. But then one hears that there are a great many properties in New Orleans on which relatively little tax is paid (I have this from a usually reliable source, but have not been able to verify the details). Now there are so many lovely homes in New Orleans that this seems very surprising, until one remembers that the tax assessor, who does the valuations, must stand for re-election every four years, and that it is the property-owners who have

[6] Koschaker, *Europa und das römische Recht* 124, 137 (4th edn., Munich and Berlin, 1966).

the votes. This is bound to affect the valuations he makes. A tax levied in such a manner cannot easily be compared with the tax assessed in Germany under the Valuation Act.

The meagre income from property taxes has a major effect on the public schools, especially as everyone in New Orleans sends his children to a private school if he can afford it, and so has no interest in raising the revenue from property taxes. Given this, can one sensibly compare public schools in the two countries? As to the standing of some city-centre schools in the United States a random remark in the *Wall Street Journal* is suggestive: in 1976 it was reported as news that children at a school were being instructed to 'Bring a note book and pen or pencil every day.'[7]

Another example while we are on schools: graduation from high-school. Children go to high-school when they are fourteen. In most public schools one never 'repeats a class' so students move up a grade every year, marks being 'curved', that is, raised as much as necessary, sometimes quite a lot. The result is that a high-school 'graduate' may have only a very slight knowledge of reading or writing. 'High-school' is an indication of age, not attainment. It is thus barely possible to compare the general run of public high-schools in the United States (unlike private schools which are often very good) with German high-schools.

This shows that our normal methods of translation are often unsuited to the United States, at any rate to the institutions of state and society with which lawyers are primarily concerned. The temptation to expect certain standards where they do not exist, or else are different, is almost irresistible—and we are forever yielding to it.

Caution, even suspicion, is in order when one is dealing with words, for language can mislead us dreadfully. Something I said earlier, and which you probably accepted, may serve as an example. In speaking of the practical uses of comparative law I alluded to the case of Switzerland.[8] But what do Swiss

[7] *Wall Street Journal*, 23 Feb. 1983, p. 1.

[8] See above ch. 2, nn. 20–3.

writers mean by 'comparative law'? Does it include only German, French, and Italian legal systems, systems with cultural and linguistic similarities? Does it extend to England, the United States, Japan, Central Africa? I suggest that the very notion of 'comparative law' may be being implicitly defined by Switzerland's geographical location, by its polyglot character, and by the languages there current. This shows that we cannot understand 'comparative law' even as an expression without knowing the cultural context.

As between English and American law language is particularly apt to mislead. The connection between them is no longer as strong as the common expression 'Anglo-American law' suggests.[9] English law is closer to German law than we think,[10] American law more distant. Shaw's quip applies here with full force: England and the United States 'are two countries separated by a common language'.[11] Or, to use American lyrics, 'Born on the other side of the sea, We are as different as people can be.'[12]

3. SPEECH REGISTERS

Even in everyday speech there are differences: in life as in law the same word may have different meanings in England and the United States. The American expression is almost always a degree more emphatic than its English counterpart.

[9] Atiyah & Summers, *Form and Substance* (above n. 1) makes clear the immense differences in American and English law and society.

[10] Gorla & Moccia, 'A "Revisiting" of the Comparison between "Continental Law" and "English Law" (16th–19th Century)', 2 *Am.J.Leg.Hist.* 143 (1981); Lawson, 'The Contribution of Roman Law to Western Civilisation', in 1 *Many Laws: Selected Essays* 124 (Amsterdam, 1977). On the influence of the Reception in England, see Baker, 'English Law and the Renaissance', 44 *Camb.L.J.* 46 (1985); Jenkins, 'English Law and the Renaissance: In Defence of Maitland', 2 *J.Leg.Hist.* 107 (1981). The influence may have been greater than had been supposed. See Moccia, 'English Law Attitudes to the "Civil Law"', 2 *J.Leg.Hist.* 157 (1981); Terrill, 'The Application of the Comparative Method by English Civilians: The Case of William Fulbeck and Thomas Ridley', 2 *J.Leg.Hist.* 169 (1981); Sherman, *Roman Law in the Modern World* (New York, 1924).

[11] Fleming, *Book Review*, 30 *Am.J.Comp.L.* 704 (1982).

[12] Rogers & Hammerstein, *South Pacific*; see also Tenney, 'English as a Dead Language', 10 *Ill.L.Rev.* 332 (1915–16).

Where the American might say 'My very best friend, my best friend, my friend' the Englishman would say 'My good friend, my friend, someone I know'. The Englishman may say he went to Oxford or Cambridge, while the American goes on about his 'alma mater' to show what a prestigious college he attended. Any distinction at school is an 'academic award'; every law school degree is a doctorate (JD). There are world championships and world fairs, and a Volkswagen dealer in the East is (naturally) 'Worldwide Volkswagen'. Beds are never of normal dimensions, always 'king-size' or 'queen-size'. The English 'policeman' becomes a 'police officer' across the Atlantic, the 'mechanic' an 'engineer'; there is a 'chamber of commerce' in every little town, and every firm has a 'President' and 'Vice-President' though it may have no other officers at all. Quite a small town may be a 'city'.

You may have noticed how readily Americans use expressions such as 'huge', 'super', 'tremendous', 'dramatic'. Often, too, an adjective is repeated: 'a beautiful, beautiful house'; indeed superlatives are sometimes duplicated, as in 'super-supreme' for a quite ordinary pizza; 'most unique', a solecism in German, is a common expression in American.

Status is important there, as it is with us. But social status is not formalized in the United States: the individual must constantly strive for it and establish his credentials. This is why self-presentation is encouraged at school, why there are awards and prizes and nominations at all levels of society, from the Oscar to the kindergarten 'super-star', the prize in the baby-contest and the accolade, for professors, of 'Teacher of the Year'.

When the Audi 100 was sold in the United States as the Audi 5000, Audi's advertisers showed that they understood this difference in speech-level: I doubt if it was fifty times as big. But it is true that a thousand million in England becomes a billion in the United States. One thing is clear: the American speech-register differs from the English. This is hardly surprising in a young and vital society. A country with such dramatic features as the Niagara Falls, the Grand Canyon, the Mojave Desert, the Great Plains, blizzards and tornadoes is going to provoke stronger reactions than England with its mild climate and manicured countryside.

Another feature which strikes us is the unembarrassed involvement of religion in everyday affairs. A Rotary Club meeting I attended started with a prayer that we might understand the person who was about to address us. And the following greeting awaited 'guests' at the Dallas Hilton: 'Because this hotel is a human institution to serve people, and not solely a money-making organization, we hope that God will grant you peace and rest while you are under our roof.' A pinch of philosophy was thrown in, too: 'We are all travelers. From birth till death we travel between the eternities.'

American society is much more geared to speech than ours; it is 'outspoken'; more energy goes in words. Statutes, contracts, and law review articles all tend to be longer there than here. Half-tones are uncommon: speak softly and you won't be heard. In the same way, the gestures of Walt Disney's creations often strike us as exaggerated.

In the result we tend to take much of what is said in the United States as being more meaningful than is intended or understood over there ('sounds good' is a characteristic delaying tactic in the United States, rather like 'let's wait and see'). It is not that there is the slightest intention to exaggerate or mislead. The fault is ours! We mistranslate because we assume that the American speech-register is the same as the English. It takes keen observation and long experience to break through the barrier of speech and recognize what is really meant by the words used.

4. LEGAL LANGUAGE

This is particularly true in law. Here too language often suggests a community of legal feeling which actually does not exist. Fleming puts it as follows:

I touched earlier on the danger of misunderstanding that can flow from superficial similarity or even identity of black-letter rules in different countries. This is especially pertinent to comparison between England and the U.S. which, to coin a phrase, are singularly divided by a common legal language. The 'official' standard of liability and proof appear the same but are worlds apart in practice because of the conservatism of professional judges on one side and 'jury lawlessness' on the other side of the Atlantic. A different example is the use of 'experts', which our author mentions without distinguishing between court-appointed experts in Europe and the parade of partisan 'oath-helpers' common to the American scene.[13]

Even the role of the attorney is quite different in England and the United States,[14] as is the doctrine of *stare decisis*, which is not really taken seriously there.[15] We should therefore stop talking of 'Anglo-American law' and treat English and American law as quite distinct. This is a first step towards avoiding error, but it is an important one.

5. DIFFERING BACKGROUNDS

There are many other ways in which the comparative lawyer may be misled. A common source of error is taking things at face value. The cultural similarities we see may be purely superficial and incidental, and we may fail to see what an American judge has called 'the radical differences between the legal systems of the United States and those of the Continent'.[16] It takes a long time for a foreigner in the United States to realize the full extent of the differences, especially outside the big cities, and he is constantly being

[13] Fleming (above n. 11); Whelan, 'On Uses and Misuses of Comparative Labour Law: A Case Study', 45 *Mod.L.Rev.* 285 (1982); Finkin, 'On "Institutional" Academic Freedom', 61 *Texas L.Rev.* 817, 822 (1983).

[14] James B. Stewart, *The Partners: Inside America's Most Powerful Law Firms* (New York, 1983).

[15] See Atiyah & Summers (above n. 1) 113–34.

[16] Aldisert, 'Rambling Through Continental Legal Systems', 43 *U.Pitts.L.Rev.* 935 (1982).

surprised.[17] For example, when a newcomer moves into a neighbourhood, it is for the established residents, not the newcomer as in Germany, to make the first visit. Comparison of eating habits as well as behaviour while visiting is also instructive. In addition, everything is subject to an almost inconceivable range of factors. To give one striking example: researchers at the State University of Colorado discovered in 1982 that the McDonald hamburger was then subject to 41,000 different regulations of federal and state origin, contained in 200 enactments and 111,000 court decisions.[18]

6. METHODS OF PAYMENT

As an example of a device which has a surprisingly different function in its different setting, let us take the cheque and credit card. 'Plastic money' is much more commonly used in the United States than in Germany. This is sometimes represented as progress, as an indication of greater economic maturity. The European visitor may have his doubts about this when he finds how long he has to wait for people to pay at the check-out counter. Why do customers put up with this, why do stores employ the extra staff? One reply is that cash may be difficult to obtain when one is away from home because the banking system is not nationally unified, and there was no way to effect a rapid transfer of funds until recently. Thus the credit card offers liquidity in an emergency. Again people are constantly on the move over there, and want a receipt for every expenditure, however small—a desire to which American tax laws conduce more than ours.

Eventually one realizes that cash is unpopular not because it is inconvenient, rather the reverse, but in part because it is dangerous. Methods of payment are affected by fear of crime in large cities. People are more aware of crime there

[17] Hyman, *The Trenton Pickle Ordinance and Other Bonehead Legislation* (1982); for Canada, see Sewell, 'Same Time Next Week', *The Globe and Mail* 10 Sept. 1983, p. 9.

[18] Center for Education and Research in Free Enterprise, Texas A & M Univ. (ed.), *Pathfinder* 3 (Dec. 1982).

than here. Crime-consciousness, taught in schools, affects a whole range of conduct too wide to instance here, though I mention the advice, constantly emphasized, never to give one's name right away on picking up the phone or to suggest that one is alone in the house, especially if one is a child. Neighbourhood watches are a common safeguard, and newly built residences often resemble bastions with a great wall and watchers at the gate.

This fear of crime is perfectly understandable. Every year in Dallas one inhabitant out of nine falls victim to a criminal attack.[19] Firearms are involved surprisingly often, on both sides. The Mayor of San Francisco lost office for trying to control the private possession of firearms. A bumper-sticker told us: 'Outlaw guns, and only outlaws will have them.' In one small town in Florida householders were urged to buy firearms and learn to use them: 'law-abiding citizens' must learn how to defend themselves in a violent society.[20] This is not typical, but it is illustrative. Another small town in Colorado actually made it part of the citizen's duty to have a firearm.[21] The 22,516 intentional homicides in the United States in 1981[22] compare with about 915 in Germany.[23]

7. THE CREDIT CARD

The European travelling in the West of the United States soon discovers that credit cards are not accepted quite as generally as the advertisements would have him believe. Some years ago the largest chain of service stations, Exxon, refused to accept any credit card, and many others charged extra. Payment with an out-of-house card is often impossible in stores and shops, in small motels, and in public places, such as National Parks.

Then why do so many people have credit cards—94 million

[19] *The Figgie Report on Fear of Crime*, Part III, 135 (Willoughby, Ohio, 1982).
[20] *FAZ* 4 June 1983, no. 127, p. 7.
[21] *FAZ* 17 May 1983, no. 113, p. 10.
[22] *Time* Magazine, 5 Sept. 1983, p. 28.
[23] Bundeskriminalamt (ed.), *Polizeiliche Kriminalstatistik 1981*, p. 56.

in 1983—and why do so many more want one, especially a major one, such as Visa or Mastercard? After all, the number of transactions per card is not very great. In 1982 there were 516 million cards but only $65 billion was charged to them.[24]

Of course when one is renting an automobile or spending a night in a motel or ordering something by telephone a credit card is convenient. But part of the answer lies in another function of the credit card which we often overlook. It serves as a personal identity card—there is no official one—and also as a status symbol: it proves that the holder has been found creditworthy, in short, that he *is* someone! It is a better means of identification than the driving licence. The credit card provides liquidity to a large extent, helps standardization where individual appraisal is impossible. Thus one has to have a credit card—and two are better than one—even if one doesn't want to use it for credit. 'Personal checks must be accompanied by one of the following valid credit cards . . .', as a notice in Holiday Inns said.

In the *Los Angeles Times* I saw an advertisement which promised to get a major credit card 'for people with credit problems'.[25] The accompanying cartoon explained: 'It wasn't credit that I was really after; I just didn't like being treated like a second class citizen.' American Express boosts its 'gold card' by saying: 'This is the charge card that says more about you than anything you can buy with it', and the Golden Mastercard is promoted as 'The ultimate recognition from your banker'.

But of course the credit card is a card for *credit*, and many people use it for that purpose: buy now, pay later. Yet credit over there is quite different from credit here. The private sector is much more 'credit-orientated' in the United States. To be deep in debt hardly enhances our standing over here,

[24] *Dallas Times Herald*, 2 Mar. 1983, p. 12.

[25] *Los Angeles Times*, 1 Aug. 1982, Part I, p. 4; In 1989 one of 'Dear Abby''s correspondents wrote: 'I guess what I hate most is being treated like a second-class citizen by rude, insensitive clerks when you tell them you don't have a credit card. They look down their noses at you as if you are a poor risk just because you don't have $8,000 of plastic debts.' *Chicago Tribune*, 29 Mar. 1989, §5 at 9.

but over there it is different: a person with no debts there cannot be creditworthy, or he would have some. Furthermore, one used to get a tax-deduction for interest payments, and, as we shall see, debtors are exposed to fewer risks. 'Enjoyment without Regret' is altogether commoner. I hope that this example of the credit card shows how cautious one must be in making comparisons in economic and legal matters with the United States.

8. THE LAW OF TORT

The law of tort provides another example of how we may be led to overlook the peculiarities of a foreign legal institution by assuming that the general framework in which it operates is much the same as in our own country. The *praesumptio similitudinis* can lead us to hasty conclusions.[26] Liability for fault, strict liability, causation, product liability and other aspects of American tort law have been avidly seized on by comparative lawyers, and they have thereby contributed to the trend to ever more extensive liability.

But have people realized that civil liability operates in a quite different social and economic context in the United States,[27] that such strong reactions may be due to greater social pressures,[28] that the social security systems are quite unalike,[29] that tort liability is often the only available instrument of social control? Have comparatists considered that the relative incidence and degree of liability cannot sensibly be discussed without taking account of the rules and practice relating to the protection of debtors, the execution of judgments, and bankruptcy?

[26] Zweigert, 'Die "Praesumptio similitudinis" als Grundsatzvermutung rechtsvergleichender Methode', in Rotondi, 2 *Inchieste di diritto comparato* 735 (Padua, 1973).

[27] Hirsch, *Law and Economics* 171 (New York, 1979).

[28] e.g. *Hurtado* v. *Superior Court of Sacramento*, 522 P.2d 666, 672 (Cal. 1974).

[29] Leibfried, 'United States and West German Welfare Systems: A Comparative Analysis', 12 *Cornell Int'l L.J.* 175 (1979).

9. ENFORCEMENT

The United States can tolerate stricter liability better than ourselves because their laws, though they vary from state to state, generally give better protection to debtors. In many states the debtor's home is exempt from execution, except for mortgages and such charges, though admittedly the home does not always form such a large part of a person's total assets as in Germany. In many states wages are non-assignable or largely so. Some states, such as Texas, are particularly favourable to debtors. But the critical point is that bankruptcy is not so much a misfortune as a 'benefit', a privilege which may be claimed every six years.[30] Bankruptcy allows a person to free himself from, to 'discharge' his liabilities, with only a few exceptions.[31] For us it is a method of execution, but there it is used to limit a debtor's liability to the current value of his effects. For us the leading characteristic of liability is that it is a clog on the future; in the United States this aspect is much less prominent.

In addition it is much easier for a debtor to evade execution by changing his name, which is always possible, or his address. Indeed every year one in five or six Americans changes his residence (16–20 per cent, as compared with our 3–4 per cent). This is a real problem in practice. In one large life-assurance company in the United States many of the policy-holders were 'orphans' who could not be 'serviced' by agents for want of a current name and address. This company admittedly did a lot of business with students, but the problem must be a general one, for a program for contacting such 'orphans' was one of the leading exhibits at an exhibition of computer assistance for insurers.

It will be seen that in the United States it is much less easy to proceed from judgment to execution than it is in Germany. If the creditor presses too hard, the debtor may well disappear, if necessary into bankruptcy. This raises a host of questions.

[30] 11 U.S.C.A. §727(a)(8).
[31] 11 U.S.C.A. §523.

Can claims arising in different countries be treated as equivalent when those countries differ so much in the execution of judgments? This may be very important when it comes to executing foreign judgments. Are we not doing more than the foreign country itself does? Should we not apply a discount on the ground that the foreign law assumes a greater slippage between judgment and execution? What about the application of foreign debtor-protection laws? Should we make a deduction because over here bankruptcy is not a 'privilege'? If we unify only the substantive law, in international sales, for instance, many important matters such as these will be left unresolved.

These questions apply to business entities, for the law of corporate reorganization and rehabilitation is very well developed in the United States. Consider the following situation, brought about by liability in tort. Could it happen here? In 1982 the Manville Corporation, the largest producer of asbestos products in the United States with a workforce of 25,000, filed under the bankruptcy laws. This was because it was being subjected to a flood of personal injury claims brought by victims of asbestos dust. Twenty thousand such claims had been brought since 1975, at a rate of 500 a month; 3,500 of them had been settled, but $660m. would be required for the remaining 16,500 claims and the firm foresaw some 32,000 further claims and costs of as much as $1.28bn. This brought the firm to its knees.[32]

The comparatist will realize that in cases of such magnitude the whole economy must answer, and that possible insurance cover is no solution. Insurance simply adds transaction costs. 'The insurance company will always lose', said Kessler of the United States,[33] a truth which is becoming evident in

[32] *Dallas Morning News*, 1 Sept. 1982, p. 15 B. As to the law, see Note, 'The Manville Bankruptcy: Treating Mass Tort Claims in Chapter 11 Proceedings', 96 *Harv.L.Rev.* 1121 (1983); Hensler, Felstiner, Selvin, & Ebener, *Asbestos in the Courts: the Challenge of Mass Toxic Torts* (Rand Corp., 1985); Reisig, 'The Man who Took on Manville', *The American Lawyer* (Jan. 1983).

[33] Kessler, 'Some Observations on the Protection of Expectations in the Private Insurance Contract in the United States', *Festschrift Zweigert* 657 (Tübingen, 1981).

Germany as well. But what about the cost of reparation? Could we meet it, as the United States does? Have we the same resources? The question hardly needs asking.[34]

10. SOCIAL ENGINEERING

Unless we take account of law in all its ramifications we are apt to reach false conclusions. So, too, with the general socio-political framework. To show this, let me take the model of the judge as 'social engineer', an American idea which has for a time been all the rage with us. What has not been sufficiently emphasized, however, is that the political and personal function and role of the judge in the United States has always been quite different from here.[35]

The courts of the United States have been a 'pillar of government'[36] since the very inception of that country, and the separation between judicature and administration has always been less clear—understandably enough, since the judge was often the only 'authority' on the spot.[37] John Marshall, great judge that he was, has been called more of a statesman than a jurist.

But we tend to forget that in the courts of the member states the judges are often elected, for a term of four to six years, mainly on clear party-political tickets and often by rather a small percentage of the electorate. Political affiliation has a great effect on the judge's career, and the press often

[34] In *In re 'Agent Orange' Product Liability Litigation* 597 F.Supp. 740 (E.D.N.Y. 1984) Judge Weinstein, approving a settlement, said 'Our country is rich in public and private resources of every kind' as a reason for holding that 'These resources should be made available . . . even though the evidence presented to the court to date suggests that the case is without merit', cited in Fleming, 'Mass Torts', [1988] *Denning L.J.* 37, 50–1.

[35] Atiyah & Summers (above n. 9) 336–58.

[36] e.g. Murphy, *The Brandeis-Frankfurter Connection: The Secret Political Activities of Two Supreme Court Justices* (New York, 1982), reviewed by Danelski, 96 *Harv.L.Rev.* 312 (1982), and Pritchet, 130 *U.Pa.L.Rev.* 1281 (1982).

[37] Haynes, 'The Language and the Logic of Law: A Case Study', 35 *U.Miami L.Rev.* 183 (1981); Aldisert (above n. 16) 993; Skiles, 'Judge Roy Bean: The Law West of the Pecos', *Texas Highways* 3 (Aug. 1982); Murphy & Rawlings, 'After the Ancient Regime: The Writing of Judgments in the House of Lords 1979–80', 44 *Mod.L.Rev.* 617 (1981), 45 *Mod.L.Rev.* 34 (1982).

mentions it in reporting his judgments. To be a state judge is often simply a step to higher political office or a reward for political services rather than a career in itself. There is thus an element of political control which we do not have in that form,[38] perhaps the counterpart of our stronger doctrinal system.

In the federal courts judges are appointed for life; they are reckoned to be better qualified and they are held in high esteem. But their nomination by the President, even at first instance, is determined by political considerations: in general one needs good political connections with Washington to become a federal judge. This applies not only to the original nomination but to the whole ladder of promotion, especially for the Supreme Court[39] ('a highly political process that brings Justices to the bench').[40] The informed lawyer always knows which President appointed which Justice (Carter-appointee, Reagan-appointee). As Shick says in his book on Judge Learned Hand, a great federal judge: 'Party affiliation and political and social conduct are usually decisive for nomination to judicial office in the lower courts, and have an effect on the conduct of the judge after nomination.'[41]

Certain constraints operate on judges in their role as social engineers,[42] and some of them operate more strongly in the United States than in Germany. One of them is the jury-system, that trial by laymen which is the hallmark of even private law in the United States. The continued existence of the jury is an expression of distrust of attorneys and judges. It is seen as the 'only defense against lawyers'.[43] 'I will even go so far as to say I think sometimes the jury

[38] Stolz, *Judging Judges* (New York, 1981).

[39] White, *Earl Warren* (New York, 1982); reviewed Kurland, 96 *Harv.L.Rev.* 331 (1982).

[40] Danelski (above n. 36).

[41] Schick, *Learned Hand's Court* 7 (Westport, 1978); Peltason, *Federal Courts in the Political Process* (New York, 1955).

[42] Neely, *Judicial Jeopardy: When Business Collides with the Courts* (1988).

[43] Schutze, 'Jury System is Only Defense against Lawyers', *Dallas Times Herald*, 12 Dec. 1982, p. B 1.

system is the only thing that stands between society and the legal profession.'[44]

Comparatists do not always make full disclosure of those factual aspects of an institution which are at odds with the legal-political value-judgements underlying their study. People in the United States do, of course, realize that the idea of the 'social engineer' is an open invitation to public and private opinion-makers of every stamp, and the idea of 'judicial restraint' [45] is gaining ground once more.[46] Neither idea encapsulates the judicial role; both, indeed, serve to camouflage particular prejudices. Words, words, words!

As to dissenting and concurring opinions, the wider legal-political context should also be taken into account in any discussion of the practice of publishing the vote of every judge. Given that judges are elected or appointed and promoted on political grounds, the dissenting opinion serves a political control function. The publication of the individual judge's view permits, and is designed to permit, reactions to it by the legal literature and the mass media,[47] sometimes with an intensity and personal directness we find shocking. There was no doubt as to this effect when certain of the mass

[44] Schutze, ibid.; see also *Colgrave* v. *Batlin*, 413 U.S. 149 (1973); Zeisel & Diamond, 'Convincing Empirical Evidence on the Six Member Jury', 41 *U.Chi.L.Rev.* 281 (1974); Gross, 'Adversaries, Juries and Justice', 26 *Loyola L.Rev.* 525 (1980).

[45] Frankfurter, 'Some Reflections on the Reading of Statutes', in Henson, *Landmarks of Law* 210 (Boston, 1960); Hirsch, *The Enigma of Felix Frankfurter* (New York, 1981), reviewed by Stone, 95 *Harv.L.Rev.* 346 (1981); Parrish, *Felix Frankfurter and His Times* (New York, 1982).

[46] Sometimes with reference to Francis Bacon: 'Judges ought to remember that their office is *jus dicere*, and not *jus dare*, to interpret the law, and not to make law, or give law. Else it will be like the authority claimed by the church of Rome, which, under pretext of exposition of Scripture, doth not stick to add and alter, and to pronounce that which they do not find, and by shew of ambiguity to introduce novelty.' Bacon, 'On Judicature', *Essays* (no. 56) (London, 1906). See also Raoul Berger, *Government by Judiciary* (Cambridge, Mass., 1977); Horwitz, *The Courts and Social Policy* (Washington, DC, 1977); Clinton, 'Judges Must Make Law: A Realistic Approach to the Judicial Function in a Democratic Society', 67 *Iowa L.Rev.* 711 (1982); Swygert, 'In Defence of Judicial Activism', 16 *Valparaiso L.Rev.* 439 (1982); 'Symposium: Court-Ordered Change in Social Institutions', 6 *Law and Human Behaviour* 97 (1982); Lücke, 'The Common Law: Judicial Impartiality and Judge-made Law', 98 *L.Q.Rev.* 29 (1982).

[47] Shapiro, 'Mr. Justice Rehnquist: A Preliminary View', 90 *Harv.L.Rev.* 293, 301 (1976).

media sharply berated the Justice who handed down the abortion decision in the Supreme Court: the judge later said that the controversy 'changed his life'.[48] The question is whether our need for secrecy in this matter is any greater. That again depends on the environment.

II. THE SOCIO-PSYCHOLOGICAL CLIMATE

This brings me to the next point. The comparative lawyer has to have at least a general sense for the socio-psychological climate in which a legal institution operates, since the significance of the institution may in great part depend on it. This 'climate' in the United States is at once more vital and harsher than ours. For example, the day after the first execution for twenty years, the *Dallas Times Herald* reported as follows under the headline 'death penalty celebration': 'It was like a birthday party in the district attorney's office on Tuesday. One attorney came in shouting that this was the greatest day in the history of Texas. Another called it the best day of his life.'[49]

These reactions indicate a sense of the need for self-defence against the growing tide of criminality, as well as the difference in speech-register noted above.

Civil lawsuits are also rather highly charged and coloured. This is how Lord Denning describes it from the English viewpoint:

> As a moth is drawn to the light, so is a litigant drawn to the United States. If he can only get his case into their courts, he stands to win a fortune. At no cost to himself, and at no risk of having to pay anything to the other side. The lawyers there will conduct the case 'on spec' as we say, or on a 'contingency fee' as they say. The lawyers will charge the litigant nothing for their services but instead they will take 40% of the damages, if they win the case in court, or out of court on a settlement. If they lose, the litigant will have

[48] Note, 'The Changing Social Vision of Justice Blackmun', 96 *Harv.L.Rev.* 717, 724 n. 47 (1983).

[49] *Dallas Times Herald*, 8 Dec. 1982, p. C 3.

nothing to pay to the other side. The courts in the United States have no such costs deterrent as we have. There is also in the United States a right to trial by jury. These are prone to award fabulous damages. They are notoriously sympathetic and know that the lawyers will take their 40% before the plaintiff gets anything. All this means that the defendant can be readily forced into a settlement. The plaintiff holds all the cards.[50]

To a German lawyer a trial by jury can be quite breathtaking. After all, the attorney who stands to win 50 per cent of the proceeds will 'go after it', 'gunning for justice'.[51] There is growing criticism of this in the United States. In 1977 Warren Burger, Chief Justice of the United States, warned that the land 'might be overrun by hordes of lawyers hungry as locusts'[52] and the Chief Justice of New York State told attorneys there that 'If lawyers just grab, grab, grab, they may be killing the goose that lays the golden egg.'[53]

12. STABILITY AND CHANGE

Another factor in the climate of legal thought is the society's predilection for stability or rapid change. Where nothing lasts long, law too may become a short-term expedient, and doctrinal consistency be rated less highly. Rapid rate of change is one feature of the United States:[54] quick short-term success is valued, people believe in 'trial and error', in the 'try it again approach'[55] which finds its classic expression in American football.

We would find it hard to match the degree of flexibility to which this gives rise. Another Dallas newspaper report was that a local justice of the peace had

[50] *Smith Kline & French* v. *Bloch*, [1983] 2 All E.R. 72, 74 (C.A.).

[51] Spence & Polk, *Gunning for Justice* (New York, 1982).

[52] *New York Times*, 28 May 1977, p. 1.

[53] Ibid. See also Gerhart, 'The Lawyer's Role in Society', *Case and Comment* 12 (July–Aug. 1982).

[54] Toffler, *Future Shock* (New York, 1970).

[55] Callmann, 'Zwei Denkmethoden im Recht: Deutschland und die Vereinigten Staaten von Amerika', in *Festschrift Möhring* 327, 332 (Munich and Berlin, 1965).

endorsed the city's proposal that his court take jurisdiction over 52,000 outstanding property-tax claims . . . having all the cases dealt with by the same court would be cheaper, even paying the court staff for overtime, than distributing the cases between different courts.[56]

Not a word about the litigant having his proper judge: any judge would do! But there was need for speed: six weeks later many of the claims would be time-barred.

Along with this flexibility there is an intermingling of public and private which we can find disconcerting. When President Carter made a state visit to Austria, he took his little daughter along; at important political pronouncements the President is often flanked by his wife. At the same time there is a wariness about public institutions, often suspected of being subject to private influence.

Much of what is said about American law can only be properly understood if one is conscious of this constant changeableness. Thus Holmes's sayings that 'The life of the law has not been logic: it has been experience'[57] or that law is simply a prediction of what the judge will decide[58] are better suited to American conditions than to cultures geared to slower development. Where everything is in rapid flux there will not be much demand for systematics or dogmatics. Thus Holmes's observations cannot be taken to apply to law as such: they are related to an American life-style and world-view. They tell us more about the United States than about law.

13. AFFLUENCE

A society's perception of itself as affluent[59] or as economical is an important factor in its Gestalt. In *People of Plenty: Economic Abundance and the American Character*,[60] Morris Potter

[56] *Dallas Times Herald*, 9 Dec. 1982, p. C 5.
[57] Holmes, *The Common Law* 1 (44th edn., Boston, 1951).
[58] Holmes, 'The Path of the Law', 10 *Harv.L.Rev.* 457, 461 (1897).
[59] Galbraith, *The Affluent Society* (Boston, 1958).
[60] (Chicago, 1954); see also Turner, *The Frontier in American History* (New York, 1920).

admirably expresses how American society is marked by the experience of wide open spaces, the sense of boundless reserves of land, of inexhaustible natural resources ('If you don't have an oil-well, just buy one'). American law is also marked by this assumption. The frontier experience still resonates, for example in the friendly 'You're welcome', now the equivalent of our 'bitte schön'. By contrast, European societies are rather founded upon the principle of economy, which again has its effects on legal doctrine. The message is that things move faster in the United States, even in law, faster than our cultural viewpoint lets us see, or want to see, or want.

14. CONCLUSION

The example of the United States shows us that comparative law has its limits and its dangers; it must be handled with care.[61] As to the method of comparative law, we have not touched upon it in all this long discussion. I just mention the key-words 'functional comparative law',[62] 'sociological comparative law'[63] and 'economic analysis of law'.[64] I have listened to what they have to say, doubtless all very worth while, but I cannot bring myself to believe that any theory is a panacea: law and comparative law are far too complex for that. We cannot embrace them from a single standpoint; method affords no security. I am more comfortable with the traditional virtues of the lawyer: observation, empathy, imagination and clarity of vision. Comparative law is no substitute for thought, indeed it can make us think about our own situation. But we must work it out for ourselves. Learn? Certainly! Imitate? Never! Every reception must be a re-creation.

[61] De Seife, 'Comparative Law: A Problem-Solving Technique', 28 *Chitty's L.J.* 60 (1980).

[62] Zweigert & Kötz, 1 *Introduction to Comparative Law* 11 (2nd edn., Oxford, 1987); less enthusiastic, Folke Schmidt, 'The Need for a Multi-Axial Method in Comparative Law', *Festschrift Zweigert* 525 (Tübingen, 1981).

[63] Heldrich, 'Sozialwissenschaftliche Aspekte der Rechtsvergleichung', 34 *RabelsZ* 427 (1970); Lawrence M. Friedman, *The Legal System: A Social Science Perspective* (Scranton, Pa., 1975).

[64] Posner, *Economic Analysis of Law* (2nd edn., Boston, 1977).

11

What Can Be Compared?

I. GENERAL CONSIDERATIONS

These considerations have brought us to the nub of comparative law: what institutions in which systems can sensibly be compared? What is of use to our own system and where can we find it? We can go only as far as time and our knowledge permit, and as we cannot say in advance how far that may be, we must comfort ourselves with G. K. Chesterton's observation that 'Art, like morality, consists in drawing the line somewhere.'

The very size of the problem has led to some abatement in the zeal which marked the beginnings of comparative law. Some people even speak of 'the law of the non-transferability of law',[1] but this is too bluntly put to be accepted, since examples of successful reception and valid unification do exist. So while we should not be unduly pessimistic, we are today more cautious in our estimate of the viability of 'legal transplants', at any rate where major cultural differences have to be bridged.[2] The hopeful hunt for 'solutions' is largely a thing of the past. Nowadays, before we make any prognosis about the transferability of law we must revisit the basic questions of comparative law, determine what it can and

[1] Hiller, 'Language, Law, Sports and Culture: The Transferability of Words, Lifestyles and Attitudes through Law', 12 *Valparaiso L.Rev.* 433 (1978); Wroblewsky, 'Problems of Incomparability in Comparative Law', 53 *Riv. int. di filosofia del diritto* 92 (1976).

[2] Watson, *Legal Transplants: An Approach to Comparative Law* (Edinburgh, 1974); Watson, 'Legal Transplants and Law Reform', 92 *Law Q.Rev.* 79 (1976); Beckström, 'Transplantation of Legal Systems: An Early Report on the Reception of Western Law in Ethiopia', 21 *Am.J.Comp.L.* 557 (1973); Beckström, 'Handicaps of Legal-Social Engineering in a Developing Nation', 22 *Am.J.Comp.L.* 697 (1974); Merryman, 'On the Convergence (and Divergence) of the Civil Law and the Common Law', 17 *Stan.J.Int'l L.* 357 (1981).

cannot do, and take proper account of the various factors which make the law what it is.[3]

Here we are still groping in the dark; to move forward at all calls for all the daring of the dilettante, mentioned earlier. Reason alone is unable to come up with a complete explanation of the nature of law, the way it develops, and whether it can be transferred.[4] The answers will often be provisional, but we must not give up. The dilemma is this: the more we try to catch the foreign law in all its individuality, as we must, the more we appreciate its cultural and societal context, the less possible it seems to compare it with others. In this way comparative law may actually obstruct the influence of foreign ideas. It is a question of finding the right balance.[5]

2. SPECIFIC FACTORS

We have seen with regard to the United States how difficult it is to grasp and describe a foreign system and its operation. To decide what law is transferable is almost more difficult. This notorious problem of comparative law is closely connected with the question of what can sensibly be compared.

It is widely supposed that the comparability of legal systems and the transferability of their institutions depend mainly on cultural, political, and economic factors, especially the power structures in state and society and on the East–West and North–South conflicts.[6] Some lay weight on the value-system

[3] Lawrence M. Friedman, *The Legal System: A Social Science Perspective* (Scranton, Pa., 1975).

[4] Sally Falk Moore, *Law as Process: An Anthropological Approach* (London, 1978); Nader & Todd (eds.), *The Disputing Process: Law in Ten Societies* (New York, 1978); Merryman (above n. 2).

[5] As Rilke says: 'The semblance of the stars, too, misleads, but for a while we are happy with what we take it to represent, and that is enough.' *Sonette an Orpheus* I. 11, in *Duinese Elegien und Sonette an Orpheus* 187 (Zurich, 1951).

[6] Kahn-Freund, 'On Uses and Misuses of Comparative Law', 37 *Mod.L.Rev.* 1, 8 (1974); McWhinney, 'Toward the Scientific Study of Values in Comparative Law Research', in *XXth Century Comparative and Conflicts Law: Essays in Honor of Hessel E. Yntema* 29 (Leiden, 1961).

of the culture in question,[7] others again on the society's conception of the individual[8] and the world. Equally important is the general 'cultural climate', resulting from the people's unconscious axioms, collective feelings, and prevalent ideas of reality. But general considerations like these hardly explain why we find it so difficult to compare our own system with that of the United States or Japan or even of England, or why we see-saw so between hope and despair. We must therefore look further afield.

First there is the question of the homogeneity of the society in question, whether it has a cultural consensus or not. Compare the United States and Japan and you will see how important this factor can be. It is closely connected with the way the law has developed in each society.[9] We have Pringsheim's word for it that 'comparative law is impossible without legal history'.[10] And it is a commonplace that the comparative lawyer has need of legal sociology[11] and legal ethnology;[12] the 'sociological dimension' of comparative law is clearly very considerable.

That said, one must immediately qualify the compliment, for there is more to law than sociology; much remains to be said when the sociologists have had their say![13] We lawyers can in our own right and from our own resources achieve *much* more than is allowed for in the hostile picture sometimes drawn of us.[14] After all if one is to embark on comparative

[7] Constantinesco, 'Ideologie als deterministisches Element zur Bildung der Rechtskreise', 19 *ZfRV* 161 (1978); Drobnig, 'The Comparability of Socialist and Non-Socialist Systems of Law', 3 *Tel Aviv Univ. Studies in Law* 45, 56 (1977).

[8] Eduard Wahl, 'Klimatische Einflüsse auf die Entwicklung des Rechts in Ost und West', in *Festschrift Möhring* 1, 6 (Munich, 1975).

[9] Presser, ' "Legal History" or the History of Law: A Primer on Bringing the Law's Past into the Present', 35 *Vand.L.Rev.* 849 (1982).

[10] Pringsheim, 'The Inner Relationship between English Law and American Law', in *Gesammelte Schriften* 76, 78 (Heidelberg, 1981); Coquillette, 'Legal Ideology and Incorporation', 61 *Boston U.L.Rev.* 1, 315 (1981), 62 *Boston U.L.Rev.* 62 (1982).

[11] Abel, 'Comparative Law and Social Theory', 26 *Am.J.Comp.L.* 219 (1978).

[12] Von Benda-Beckmann, 'Ethnologie und Rechtsvergleichung', 67 *Archiv für Rechts-und Sozialphilosophie* 310 (1981).

[13] Leff, 'Economic Analysis of Law: Some Realism About Nominalism', 60 *Va.L.Rev.* 451 (1974).

[14] Campbell & Wiles, 'The Study of Law in Society', in Evan (ed.), *The Sociology of Law* 3 (New York, 1980); Catterrell, 'Jurisprudence and Sociology of Law', ibid. at 21.

law or legal sociology one must first be a *lawyer*. The observation of legal interrelationships and the study of legal institutions can save a lot of field-work, for law, at least when one includes history, is a 'mirror of society',[15] even if sometimes a dark one. And who better to handle this mirror than lawyers, professionally accustomed to dimming and deeming? Lawyers can also learn from the absence of a particular legal institution, for there are reasons for absence as well as presence. But in general if we are to ascertain the actual effect of legal solutions, co-operation between all relevant disciplines is required.[16]

But even this is not enough, for there are several very important factors not yet mentioned which have a great influence on the law. They are obvious enough—the natural environment, the size of the state and its geographical situation, its climate, the fertility of its soil, its natural resources, ease of movement, density of population, and level of welfare. We have already glanced at some of these factors in the American example. To these we must add language and religion.

These factors are particularly important for comparative law; it is often differences in geography, language, and religion that we first notice, especially on leaving Europe, and they can open our eyes to factors which have affected the substance of law within our own cultural circle. Their effect naturally varies as between the different areas of law, but it is hard to identify its precise extent in any particular case because the influence of other factors is very difficult to isolate.

[15] Schmitthoff, 'Die künftige Aufgaben der Rechtsvergleichung', *JZ* 1978, 495.

[16] Carbonnier, 'L'Apport du droit comparé à la sociologie juridique', in *Livre du Centenaire de la société de législation comparée* 75 (Paris, 1969).

12

Geography and Law

I. INTRODUCTION

Montesquieu noted that geography exerted a major influence on law, and observed that this geographical and climatic character of legal rules was a major obstacle to their transfer from one country to another.[1] Pascal was rather sarcastic on the subject:

> The quality of everything as just or unjust changes with the climate. Three degrees of latitude to the North, and all jurisprudence is stood on its head; truth is determined by longitude . . . It is surely peculiar that justice should end at a river! Or that a thing be true on one side of the Pyrenees and false on the other.[2]

Since then we have rather lost sight of the extent to which law depends on geography, despite the work of Ehrlich.[3] This is in part because the natural preconditions and constraints to which every legal system is subject have been rather obscured by increased travel, advances in technology, and the industrial revolution, but they are coming to the forefront again now that we are so conscious of the need to protect the environment. Not long ago, when Zimmermann was Minister of the Interior, he announced that Germany was not going to follow the United States and Japan in making lead-free gasoline mandatory. This was because Germany, unlike both the continental United States and insular Japan, had to take account of the movement of vehicles from neighbouring

[1] Montesquieu, 1 *De l'esprit des lois* 239–285 (Bks. 14–16) (ed. Truc, Paris, 1956). There had been previous hints in Plato, *Laws* Bk. 4, 704–7, Bk. 5, 747, in Taylor (trans.), *Laws of Plato* 87–90, 130 (London, 1934), Aristotle, *Politics* 208 f. (Zurich, 1955), and Bodin, *Six Books of The Commonwealth* 145–57 (ed. and trans. Tooley, Oxford, n.d.).

[2] Pascal, *Pensées* no. 230, p. 80 (ed. Chevalier, Paris, 1937), taken from Montaigne, 2 *Essais* 287 (ed. Rat, Classiques Garnier, Paris, 1952).

[3] Ehrlich, *Grundlegung der Soziologie des Rechts* 408 (Munich 1913). Ehrlich invokes Le Play, *Les ouvriers européens* (2nd edn., Tours, 1879).

countries: different rules because of differences in geography.

Important work on geography and law has recently been done by Neumann-Duesberg[4] and Eduard Wahl,[5] taking up the Japanese writer, Tetsuro Watsuji.[6] Hans Baade has applied these and cognate ideas in the field of constitutional law.[7] Langhans-Ratzeburg also deserves a mention; he coined the word 'Geojurisprudence' in 1928, but was mainly interested in drawing a legal atlas;[8] so does Merk, who two years previously had spoken of 'legal geography'.[9]

2. MORE DETAIL

The culture and law of a country are as dependent on its geography as is its very terrain. A good example is the fact that the Moors in Spain never settled north of the forty-first parallel, beyond which olives would not grow.[10] Other examples are the legal devices adopted to deal with scarcities due to geographical factors. The fact that law is affected by its geographical setting may make it harder or easier to import, as is perfectly obvious in extreme cases such as the laws of the Eskimos[11] or the Bedouin. The Supreme Court of the Philippines once well said that law often 'takes on a different colour in a different environment'.[12]

I became conscious of this in Cambridge, speaking to Kurt

[4] Neumann-Duesberg, *Sprache im Recht* 20 (Münster, 1949).

[5] Eduard Wahl, 'Klimatische Einflüsse auf die Entwicklung des Rechts in Ost und West', *Festschrift Möhring* 1 (Munich, 1975).

[6] Tetsuro Watsuji, *A Climate* (Tokyo, 1961); cf. Djuvara, *Civilisation et lois historiques* (Paris, 1975); von Bar, 'Die Entwicklung des südafrikanischen Zivilrechts dargestellt an Fragen des Haftungsrechts', 42 *RabelsZ* 87, 98 (1978); Noda, *Introduction to Japanese Law* 58 (Tokyo, 1976).

[7] Baade, *Das Verhältnis von Parlament und Regierung im Bereich der auswärtigen Gewalt der Bundesrepublik Deutschland* 19, 21 (Hamburg, 1962).

[8] Langhans-Ratzeburg, *Begriff und Aufgaben der geographischen Rechtswissenschaft* (*Geojurisprudenz*) (Berlin-Grünewald, 1928).

[9] Walter Merk, *Wege und Ziele der geschichtlichen Rechtsgeographie* (Berlin, 1926).

[10] Previté-Orton, 1 *Shorter Cambridge Medieval History* 372 (Cambridge, 1966).

[11] Hoebel, *The Law of Primitive Man: A Study in Comparative Legal Dynamics* 67 (Cambridge, Mass., 1964).

[12] *Javellana* v. *Mirasol & Nuane*, 40 Philippine Reports 761, 775 (Sup.Ct. 1920).

Lipstein about how and why English law is so 'different'. 'You must remember,' he said, 'there is always the Channel,' and it is true that English law is still distinctly characterized by its insularity, notwithstanding the influence of Roman Law and the European *ius commune* in the Middle Ages.[13] English law is also characterized by the centralization which the Normans instituted so early, itself a consequence of London's strategic location.[14] Even clearer is the effect of insularity upon Japanese law.[15]

Is there any general principle behind these instances? When anthropologists tell us that man has always been a territorial animal,[16] we are put in mind of the territorial principle in modern law. In low-lying countries the rule was 'Wer nicht will deichen, muss weichen' ('Dike or drown'); places exposed to earthquake or hurricane have special building regulations; sunny and cloudy countries have different rules about light and the minimum requisite distance between buildings—compare Naples and Hamburg. Other effects of geography on law can be seen by considering what happened to English law when it emigrated to the United States.[17]

3. WATER LAW

Water law can serve as our example. The attempt to apply the water law of a country as wet as England was bound to

[13] Coquillette, 'Legal Ideology and Incorporation', 61 *Boston U.L.Rev.* 1, 315 (1981), 62 *Boston U.L.Rev.* 62 (1982); Ehrenzweig, *Psychoanalytische Rechtswissenschaft* 127 (Berlin, 1973).

[14] North, 'Problems of Codification in a Common Law System', 46 *RabelsZ* 490 (1982).

[15] Kim & Lawson, 'The Law of the Subtle Mind', 28 *I.C.L.Q.* 491, 492 (1979).

[16] Abbas, 'Earliest Hunters Staked Out Boundaries', *Forum—Southern Methodist University* (no. 3, Feb. 1983); Cashdan, 'Territoriality among Human Foragers: Ecological Models and an Application to Four Bushman Groups', 24 *Current Anthropology* 47 (1983); Wohlwill & Wasman, *The Physical Environment and Behavior: An Annotated Bibliography* 152 (New York, 1981).

[17] Bakken, *The Development of Law on the Rocky Mountain Frontier: Civil Law and Society 1850–1912* (Westport, Conn., 1983); Horwitz, *The Transformation of American Law 1780–1860* (Cambridge, Mass., 1977); cf. Williams, 25 *U.C.L.A.L.R.* 1187 (1978); Winship, 31 *Sw.L.J.* 751 (1977); Holt, 'Morton Horwitz and the Transformation of American Legal History', 23 *Wm. & Mary L.Rev.* 663 (1982); Roscoe Pound, 'The Development of American Law and its Deviation from English

give rise to social tensions in the arid American South-West and eventually to a change in the law itself.[18] Let us follow the development. In lieu of the Common Law's 'riparian theory' which gave the riparian owner a prior right to water, the West and South-West of the United States adopted the 'law of appropriation', which favoured the person who first exploited or made 'reasonable use' of the water: first in time, first in right. The reasons for the change were given by the Supreme Court of Colorado in 1882:

> The climate is dry, and the soil, when moistened only by the usual rainfall, is arid and unproductive; except in a few favored sections, artifical irrigation for agriculture is an absolute necessity. Water in the various streams thus acquires a value unknown in moister climates . . . Deny the doctrine of priority or superiority of right by priority of appropriation, and a great part of the value of all this property is at once destroyed. . . . We conclude, then, that the common law doctrine giving the riparian owner a right to the flow of water in its natural channel upon and over his lands, even though he makes no beneficial use thereof, is inapplicable to Colorado. Imperative necessity, unknown to the countries which gave it birth, compels the recognition of another doctrine in conflict therewith.[19]

Comparable change took place in the right to abstract water from one's own property. In 'England's green and pleasant land'[20] the rule was that one could take as much as one chose.[21] In the United States this was changed, and the

Law', 67 *L.Q.Rev.* 49 (1951); Kahn-Freund, 'English Law and American Law: Some Comparative Reflections', in Newman (ed.), *Essays in Jurisprudence in Honor of Roscoe Pound* 362 (Indianapolis, 1962).

[18] Wiel, 'Fifty Years of Water Law', 50 *Harv.L.Rev.* 252 (1936); Williams, 'Optimizing Water Use: The Return Flow Issue', 44 *U.Colo.L.Rev.* 301 (1973). For comprehensive treatment, see Horwitz (above n. 17). For a modern variant, see Comment, 'The Allocation of Sunlight: Solar Rights and the Prior Appropriation Doctrine', 47 *U.Colo.L.Rev.* 421 (1976); Williams, 'Solar Access and Property Rights: A Maverick Analysis', 11 *Conn.L.Rev.* 430 (1979). On wind energy, see Taubenfeld, 'Wind Energy: Legal Issues and Legal Barriers', 21 *Sw.L.J.* 1053 (1978).

[19] *Coffin* v. *Left Hand Ditch Co.*, 6 Colo. 443, 446–447 (1879).

[20] William Blake, 'Jerusalem'; *City of Pleasanton* v. *Lower Nueces River Supply Dist.*, 263 S.W.2d 797, 800 (Tex.App. 1953).

[21] *Acton* v. *Blundell*, 12 M. & W. 324, 152 Eng.Rep. 1223 (1843).

predominant rule today is that of 'reasonable use' and 'correlative right': water may be abstracted only for proper purposes and with due regard for the effect of such abstraction on neighbouring land.[22]

4. STRICT LIABILITY

But the influence of geography goes much further. It explains, for example, why Texas refused to adopt the English rule of *Rylands* v. *Fletcher*,[23] whereby the occupier of land is strictly liable for damage done by the escape of water which he has brought on to it. In 1936 the Supreme Court of Texas said:

> In *Rylands* v. *Fletcher* the court predicated the absolute liability of the defendants on the proposition that the use of land for the artificial storage of water was not a natural use, and that, therefore, the landowner was bound at his peril to keep the waters on his own land. . . . The basis of the English rule is to be found in the meteorological conditions which obtain there. England is a pluvial country, where constant streams and abundant rains make the storage of water unnecessary for ordinary or general purposes.

In Texas the situation was different:

> In Texas we have conditions very different from those which obtain in England. A large portion of Texas is an arid or semi-arid region. West of the 98th meridian of longitude, where the rainfall is approximately 30 inches, the rainfall decreases until finally, in the extreme western part of the state, it is only about ten inches. This land of decreasing rainfall is the great ranch or livestock region of the state, water for which is stored in thousands of ponds, tanks, and lakes on the surface of the ground. The country is almost without streams; and without the storage of water from rainfall in basins constructed for the purpose, or to hold waters pumped from the earth, the great livestock industry of West Texas must perish. No such condition obtains in England. With us the storage of water is a natural or necessary and common use of land . . . the rule

[22] *City of Corpus Christi* v. *City of Pleasanton*, 276 S.W.2d 798, 801 (Tex. 1955); *Basset* v. *Salisbury Mfg. Co.*, 43 N.H. 569 (1862).

[23] *Rylands* v. *Fletcher*, (1868) L.R. 3 H.L. 330.

announced in Rylands v. Fletcher, predicated upon different conditions, can have no application here.

The Court adduced the further argument that Texas was a producer of mineral oil:

Again, in England there are no oil wells, no necessity for using surface storage facilities for impounding and evaporating salt waters therefrom. In Texas the situation is different. Texas has a great many oil fields, tens of thousands of wells in almost every part of the state. Producing oil is one of our major industries. One of the by-products of oil production is salt water, which must be disposed of without injury to property or the pollution of streams. The construction of basins or ponds to hold this salt water is a necessary part of the oil business.[24]

5. FENCING IN, FENCING OUT

An even more dramatic instance of the effect of geography on law is the 'fencing problem': are cattle to be fenced out or fenced in?[25] This was the *casus belli* between ranchers and farmers in the West and South-West (Texas) of the United States: it is the classic Cain–Abel conflict.

The traditional rule at common law was that the owner of cattle had to fence his cattle in, or pay for any harm his beasts did in his neighbour's fields.[26] This rule was appropriate enough in a densely populated country with an economic interest in protecting intensive farming, but the different geographical conditions in the Mid- and South-West of the United States turned this 'fencing in' rule inside out: it became a rule of 'fencing out'.[27]

[24] *Turner* v. *Big Lake Oil Co.*, 96 S.W.2d 221, 225 ff. (Tex. 1936); see also Prosser, 'The Principle of *Rylands* v. *Fletcher*', in *Selected Topics on the Law of Torts* 135, 149 (Ann Arbor, 1953).

[25] Meinig, *Imperial Texas: An Interpretative Essay in Cultural Geography* (Austin, 1969). The case was used by Coase in developing his theorem: 'The Problem of Social Cost', 3 *J. L. & Comm.* 1 (1960). See now Vogel, 'The Coase Theorem and California Animal Trespass Law', 16 *J.Leg.Stud.* 149 (1987). I am most grateful to Prof. Joseph McKnight of the Southern Methodist University Law School for letting me see his collected materials.

[26] Glanville Williams, *Liability for Animals* (Cambridge, 1939).

[27] Ingham, *The Law of Animals* 258 (Philadelphia, 1900).

Some of the judgments give detailed reasons for the change. Thus in 1848 the Supreme Court of Illinois said:

> However well adapted the rule of the common law may be to a densely populated country like England, it surely is but ill adapted to a new country like ours. If this common law rule prevails now, it must have prevailed from the time of the earliest settlements in the State, and can it be supposed that when the early settlers of this country located upon the borders of our extensive prairies, that they brought with them and adopted as applicable to their condition a rule of law, requiring each one to fence up his cattle; that they designed the millions of fertile acres stretched out before them to go ungrazed, except as each purchaser from the government was able to inclose his part with a fence? This State is unlike any of the eastern States in their early settlement, because, from the scarcity of timber, it must be many years yet before our extensive prairies can be fenced, and their luxuriant growth sufficient for thousands of cattle must be suffered to rot and decay where it grows, unless the settlers upon their borders are permitted to turn their cattle upon them.[28]

The court held that 'the common-law rule does not and never has prevailed in Illinois'.[29]

This meant that the farmer who wanted to protect his fields had to build a fence round them. The Supreme Court of Kansas stated: 'The owner of real estate does not use reasonable and ordinary care and diligence to protect his property from the intrusion of roaming cattle unless he incloses it with a lawful fence.'[30] The matter was summed up in 1890 by the Supreme Court of the United States: the rule which rendered the rancher liable

> . . . was ill adapted to the nature and condition of the country at that time. Owing to the scarcity of means for inclosing lands, and the great value of the use of the public domain for pasturage, it was never adopted or recognized as the law of the country. . . . Indeed, it is only within a few years past, as the country has been

[28] *Seeley* v. *Peters*, 10 Ill.Rep. (Gilman) 130, 143 (1848).
[29] Ibid.
[30] *Union Pac. Ry.* v. *Rollins*, 5 Kan.Rep. 167, 177 (1869).

settled and become highly cultivated, all the land nearly being so used by its owners or by their tenants, that the question of compelling the owner of cattle to keep them confined has been the subject of agitation.[31]

For the cowboys who needed to drive their cattle to water-holes and to eastern markets it was essential that the land remain unfenced, so against the background of the 'fence-cutters' struggle for the open prairie, many 'fencing-statutes' were enacted in the prairie states.[32] Another product is the folk-song *Don't fence me in*: 'Oh give me land, lots of land, under the starry sky above, Don't fence me in.'[33]

The law varied somewhat from state to state.[34] But increasingly, as the Supreme Court of the United States indicated, there was a trend back to 'fencing in' because of population growth and the move from pasture to farmland. But it was technical developments which were determinative. The wood needed for making the fences could now be brought into the prairie by railroad; barbed wire,[35] invented in the 1870s, made it possible to fence large areas stoutly enough to withstand even the savage 'longhorns', which were gradually replaced by less undomesticated strains; the windwheel brought water to the surface where drovers could reach it without crossing other people's land. The memory of the struggle lingers on, as in the song in Rodgers and Hammerstein's *Oklahoma*:

[31] *Buford* v. *Houtz*, 133 U.S. 320, 328 (1890); *Lazarus* v. *Phelps*, 152 U.S. 81 (1894); *Garcia* v. *Sumrall*, 121 P.2d 640, 645 (Ariz. 1942): '. . . if the old common law rule of trespass was applied, it would have been practically impossible to use these federal lands for grazing, for the animals roaming at large thereon, due to their natural instincts, would be practically certain to trespass upon any privately owned lands lying adjacent to the open range.'

[32] *Ford* v. *Taggert*, 4 Tex.Rep. 492 (1849); *Clarendon Land Inv. & Ag. Co.* v. *McClelland*, 34 S.W. 98, reh. den. 35 S.W. 474 (Tex. 1896); Prosser, Wade & Schwarz, *Cases and Materials on Torts* 707 (ed. 7, Minneola, N.Y., 1982).

[33] Conrad Richter, *The Sea of Grass* (1937).

[34] Ingham (above n. 27) 265.

[35] McCallum, *The Wire that Fenced the West* (Norman, Okla., 1965); Kalez, 'Barbed Wire Benny', *The Cattleman* (Jan. 1972) 50; Gates, 'The Devil's Rope', *Texas Highways* 24 (Sept. 1982).

The farmer and the cowman should be friends!
Oh the farmer and the cowman should be friends!
The one man likes to push a plow,
The other likes to chase a cow,
But that's no reason why they can't be friends.

Anyone tempted to treat this as just another American oddity not to be taken seriously will be disconcerted to find that Texas had the rule of 'fencing out' when it was still under Spanish sovereignty.[36] The conclusion is not that American law modelled itself on Spanish law: it is that geography was more powerful than legal culture or history.[37]

6. CONCLUSION

These few examples must suffice for the topic 'Geography and Law', but they could be multiplied. We might note that the see-saw between the rival theories of domicile and incorporation in international company law has a geographical basis—continental Europe v. insular England; so too with the varieties of company law (Liechtenstein and Delaware) and for the different tax systems (income tax or sales tax). 'Tax-havens' and 'off-shore banking' are terms which identify the relevant law by reference to its geographical location. The experience of wide open spaces, the sense of inexhaustible reserves of land is, as we have already noted, a load-bearing element of American law. The denser the population, the greater the need for legal protection of the private sphere and for formality, which is the bulwark of freedom.[38] Rules of conduct and conduct itself are bound to differ depending on whether there are 639 people per square mile, as in West Germany, or only 65 as in the United States.

[36] Myres, *The Ranch in Spanish Texas 1691–1800*, 25 (1969).

[37] Jordan, 'The Origin of Anglo-American Cattle Ranching in Texas: A Diffusion from the Lower South', 45 *Economic Geography* 63 (1969).

[38] Margulis, 'Privacy as a Behavioral Phenomenon', 33 *J.Soc.Issues* 1 (1977); *In Re Dinnan*, 661 F.2d 426 (11th Cir. 1981); *Gray* v. *Board of Higher Education*, 692 F.2d 901 (2d Cir. 1982); Finkin, 'On Judicially Compelled Disclosures', *Academe* 181 (1981).

For the comparative lawyer the question which poses itself is this: how does law change when you move it into a different geographical environment? We are just beginning to answer this question, which poses a heavy task for comparative law.

13

Language and Law

I. INTRODUCTION

It may seem paradoxical to say that comparative lawyers have only recently discovered how important a factor language is.[1] After all, they obviously have to know some languages, and must realize that language and law belong together, that language is *the* tool of the lawyer. In terms of personalities law and language have certainly gone together: Jacob Grimm, whose *Deutsche Grammatik*[2] is the foundation of scientific German philology, was a lawyer, and so was Ludwig Reiners, author of *Deutsche Stilkunst*,[3] joined more recently by the *Unwörterbuch* of Gleiss,[4] yet another lawyer. Language has often cropped up in this very book, language as register, language as embellishment, language as camouflage.[5] If 'Law

[1] Basic works are Holldack, *Grenzen der Erkenntnis ausländischen Rechts* 82 ff. (Leipzig, 1919); Dölle, *Vom Stil der Rechtssprache* (Tübingen, 1945). See also Wassermann & Petersen, *Recht und Sprache* (Heidelberg, 1983); Hiller, 'Language, Law, Sports and Culture: The Transferability of Words, Lifestyles and Attitudes through Law', 12 *Valparaiso U.L.Rev.* 433 (1978); Seidemann, 'The Communication of Law and the Process of Development', [1972] *Wis.L.Rev.* 686; Stone, 'From a Language Perspective', 90 *Yale L.J.* 1149 (1981); Olivecrona, 'Legal Language and Reality', in Newman (ed.), *Essays in Jurisprudence in Honor of Roscoe Pound* 151 (Indianapolis, 1962); London (ed.), *The World of Law* (New York, 1960); Weinberg, 'Law and Literature', 5 *Trial Diplomacy Journal* 4 (no. 4, 1982–3); 'Symposium—Law and Literature', 60 *Texas L.Rev.* 373 (1982). See also Mellinkoff, *The Language of the Law* (Boston, 1963); Mellinkoff, *Legal Writing: Sense and Nonsense* (St Paul, 1982); Philbrick, *Language and the Law* (New York, 1949); Block, 'What did you Say? What did you Mean?', 28 *J.Leg.Ed.* 542 (1977); Shapiro, *Probability and Certainty in Seventeenth-Century England: A Study of the Relationship between Natural Science, Religion, History, Law and Literature* (Princeton, 1983); Peter Goodrich, *Legal Discourse: Studies in Linguistics, Rhetoric and Legal Analysis* (London, 1987); Kevelson, 'Semiotics and Structures of Law', 35 *Semiotica* 183 (1987).

[2] (4 vols., Göttingen, 1819–37).

[3] (Munich, 1943).

[4] (Frankfurt, 1982).

[5] Edelmann, *Politics as Symbolic Action* (Chicago, 1971); Noonan, *Persons and Masks of the Law* (New York, 1976); George Orwell, 'Politics and the English Language', in 4 *Collected Essays, Journalism and Letters of George Orwell* 127–40 (ed. S. Orwell & Angus, London, 1968); Austin, 'Performative-Constative', in Searle

shows itself in a mask',[6] the mask is language; and if, as Kipling said, language is the 'mightiest drug' of mankind, it is a drug with legal side-effects.[7]

But we must pursue the question, and ask how law may be influenced by its particular language, by its vocabulary, its structure, and its grammar. Is there any connection between legal and linguistic structures? If so, how intimate a connection is it? What happens when you translate a legal institution into a different language? Some research has been done into the changes which occurred in ex-colonial legal systems in Africa and Asia when English gave way to native languages,[8] but I do not know of any studies of the change from Latin to German in this country or the change in the language of the church. As to the church the question may be less important, since the true language of the Catholic church is the liturgy. Systematic studies of law and language have been made by Forsthoff and especially Neumann-Duesberg,[9] and in the Netherlands and Belgium by Van den Bergh and Broekman;[10] for England Glanville Williams should be mentioned;[11] but these works have not yet borne much fruit in comparative law.

2. MORE DETAIL

'Language is the mother of thought, not its maid.' Karl Kraus's apophthegm is a good start for our consideration of

(ed.), *The Philosophy of Language* 13 (Oxford, 1971); James Boyd White, 'Law as Rhetoric, Rhetoric as Law: The Arts of Cultural and Communal Life', 52 *Chi.L.Rev.* 684 (1985).

[6] Bentham, cited by Hart, *Esssays on Bentham* 2 (Oxford, 1982). See also, on 'jargonization', *Rationale of Judicial Evidence* Book 8, Ch. 17, in Bowring (ed.), 7 *Works of Jeremy Bentham* 280 (Edinburgh, 1843).

[7] Neumann-Duesberg, *Sprache im Recht* 88 (Münster, 1949).

[8] Marasinghe, 'The Social Consequences of Legal Language Switch-Overs in Sri Lanka', 1 *Lawasia* 74 (1979); Marasinghe, 'Some Problems Associated with a Language Switch-Over in the Third World', 10 *Verfassung und Recht in Übersee* 507 (1977).

[9] Forsthoff, *Recht und Sprache* (Halle (Saale), 1940); Neumann-Duesberg (above n. 7).

[10] Van den Bergh & Broekman, *Recht en Taal* (Deventer, 1979).

[11] Glanville Williams, 'Language and the Law', 61 *L.Q.Rev.* 71, 179, 293 (1945), 62 *L.Q.Rev.* 387 (1946).

the relationship between language and thought. No less disconcerting are the sayings of Stefan George, 'When words fail, no thing remains,' and Heidegger, 'Only in word and language do things come into and remain in being.'[12] I can do no more than touch upon the connections thus adumbrated.[13]

Kantorowicz called jurisprudence a 'word science', and Roscoe Pound adopted his expression.[14] What are we to understand by it? We approach the matter by noting the importance in ancient law of rhythm, alliteration, and rhyme, and even verse. The links between poetry and law have always surprised me: the very symbol we use for the paragraphs of the BGB (§) comes to us from Greek tragedy. Then we have Jacob Grimm on *Poetry in Law*,[15] Erik Wolff on *Law in German Poetry*,[16] and Wohlhaupter's *Poet-Lawyers*.[17] Hölderlin's *Hyperion* had a tremendous impact on Savigny, as did much other German literature, romantic and classical. There is also a very strong connection between law and fairy-tales, such as Grimm's *Tischchen deck dich, Goldesel und Knüppel aus dem Sack*. Is all this just coincidence—or is it something more?

Another approach is to consider the technical legal language used for imported law. Law French, the language adopted by the medieval English from the Norman invaders, provides a good example. This specialist language helped to prevent as complete a reception of Roman law as occurred on the continent:

[12] Heidegger, *Einführung in die Metaphysik* 11 (2nd edn., Tübingen, 1958).

[13] Briskin & Stone, *Law, Language and Ethics* (Minneola, NY, 1972). Cf. Stalin, *Der Marxismus und die Fragen der Sprachwissenschaft* (Stuttgart, 1953).

[14] Pound, 'Some Thoughts about Comparative Law', 1 *Festschrift Rabel* 7 (Tübingen, 1954); Danet, 'Language in the Legal Process', 14 *Law & Soc'y Rev.* 455, 540 (1979–80); Berman, 'The Religious Foundations of Western Law', 24 *Cath.U.L.Rev.* 490, 502 (1975).

[15] Jacob Grimm, 'Von der Poesie im Recht', 2 *Zeitschrift für geschichtliche Rechtswissenschaft* 25 (1816).

[16] Erik Wolf, *Vom Wesen des Rechts in deutscher Dichtung* (Frankfurt, 1946). See also Fehr, *Das Recht in der Dichtung* (Berne, 1931).

[17] Wohlhaupter, *Dichterjuristen* (3 vols., Tübingen, 1953). For law and the plastic arts, see Fehr, *Kunst und Recht* (Zurich, 1923).

English law was tough and impervious to foreign influence because it was highly technical, and it was highly technical because English lawyers had been able to make a vocabulary, to define their concepts, to think sharply as the man of science thinks.[18]

We should recall the close historical connection between law and rhetoric in the Glossators, between scholasticism and jurisprudence, and again between law and poetry. The links occur through the medium of language: 'Rhetoric is in turn the child of the myths and poetry . . . The poetry and myths are the response of a prehistoric people to the universe around them.'[19]

We should not be surprised to learn how legal thinking is shaped by its technical jargon,[20] as James B. White shows in *The Legal Imagination*.[21] What effect will data-processing have on our law? This question brings us back to our main theme: if legal language affects the thinking of lawyers, is the effect of language on law a general one? The implications for comparative law will be obvious.

3. LANGUAGE AS A CREATIVE FORCE

Let us start cautiously, right at the beginning, with Adam and Eve. You will remember that in Genesis it says: 'And Adam gave names to all cattle, and to the fowl of the air, and to every beast of the field . . .'[22]

Language is the means by which he recognized the creatures, it gave him access to the world, to reality. The same point, but in reverse, is made in the dealings between God and Jacob and Moses: God will not give his name, he is not to

[18] Maitland, 1 *Year Books of Edward II (1307–1309)* xxxvi (London, 1903; Selden Society Reprints vol. 17, Year Book Series vol. 1), cited in White, *The Legal Imagination* 6 (Boston, 1973).

[19] Pirsig, *Zen and the Art of Motorcycle Maintenance* 391 (New York, 1974).

[20] Eisele, 'The Legal Imagination and Language: A Philosophical Criticism', 57 *U.Colo.L.Rev.* 363 (1976); Danet, 'Language in the Legal Process', 14 *Law & Soc'y Rev.* 445 (1979–80); Conley, O'Barr, & Lind, 'The Power of Language: Presentational Style in the Courtroom', [1978] *Duke L.J.* 1375.

[21] (Boston, 1973).

[22] Gen. 2: 20.

be caught or dominated.[23] For the same reason the name of the chief of the Gods of Rome was a secret. We find the same idea in *The Odyssey*, when the 'cruel monster' Polyphemus says to Odysseus 'Tell me your name' and receives the reply 'My name is No one, for no one is what everyone calls me,'[24] and in Wagner's *Lohengrin*: 'Never ask me nor worry yourself whence I come or what my name and nature.'[25]

If we now bring into account the opening of St John's Gospel, 'In the beginning was the word', and remember that in many religious mythologies the 'word' is ontologically supreme[26]—then we can begin to see the power that language exercises over us. The Bambara in West Africa, for example, believe that words and things coalesce:

> This means that things had implicitly been designated and named before they came into existence, and that they are called into existence by their name and designation. But they were not known as such except in the consciousness of man, the '(seed)corn' or origin of the universe.[27]

According to this belief, it is through the 'word' that things obtain their existence. In the Bible, too, the act of creation takes verbal form: 'And God said, "Let there be light!" '[28] and 'God said "Let there be a firmament in the midst of the waters" '[29] and so on. The *fiat* had to be *said*. At Whitsun, too, the 'Creator Spiritus' manifested itself in the gift of tongues, a miracle of speech.[30] There is a highly relevant passage also in Goethe's *Faust*.[31]

[23] Gen. 32: 30; Exod. 3: 14.

[24] Homer, *Odyssey*, 10. 366.

[25] Wagner, *Lohengrin* I. iii, in Wagner, 2 *Werke* 162 (Frankfurt, 1983); so also in Wolfram von Eschenbach, *Parzival*, §825 l. 18 in Wolfram von Eschenbach, 3 *Werke* 195 (5th edn., Leitzmann, Tübingen, 1960).

[26] Cassirer, *Language and Myth* 44 (New York, 1946).

[27] Dieterlin, *Essai sur la religion Bambara* (Paris, 1951), cited in Schott, 'Der gegessene Gott: Mensch und Kosmos in afrikanischen Weltbildern', in 4 *Schriftenreihe der Westfälischen Wilhelms-Universität Münster* 89, 92 (1982).

[28] Gen. 1: 3.

[29] Gen. 1: 6.

[30] Acts 2: 3.

[31] Part I, Studierzimmer: 'Geschrieben steht: Im Anfang war das *Wort*. . . . Und schreib getrost: Im Anfang war die *Tat*!'

Perhaps we can pause for a moment, and consider how the word 'verb' which originally meant just 'word' is now our primary 'activity word'. Does this not tell us something about the creative power of the word? Again, the word 'poet' means 'creator', 'maker'. This ties in nicely with the discovery in linguistics that the characteristic feature of language is its astonishing creative power: the child can compose and understand sentences it has never heard before. Indeed there is no limit to the number of sentences we can form and understand.[32]

4. NAME AND WORD MYTHS

We have seen how the use of a person's name makes him present, calls him into being. This is a frequent phenomenon. Back to the Bible: 'I have called thee by thy name: thou art mine.'[33] The ritual words when a person receives a blessing or crosses himself are 'In the name of the Father . . .'. Again, from St Matthew, '. . . where two or three are gathered together in my name, there am I in the midst of them.'[34] The name gives existence; the name and the person are one.

In the popular domain we recall the story of Rumpelstiltzkin ('How good it is that no one knows | That my name "Rumpelstiltzkin" goes') and also the old German song 'God the Father used their name, | And thus they into being came.'

This shows that 'A person who knew the right words and used them correctly was in possession of the things themselves and could dispose of them as he wished.'[35] Rilke gives poetic expression to the idea in 'Ich fürchte mich so vor der Menschen Wort.'

If there are many examples of the creative power of language in the religious context, such as the sacral words in

[32] Skinner, Book Review of Chomsky, 35 *Language* 26 (1959).

[33] Isa. 43: 1.

[34] Matt. 18: 20.

[35] Neumann-Duesberg (above n. 7) 24.

baptism or in the transubstantiation of the Mass ('hoc est corpus meum' retained its magic power even when garbled into 'hocus-pocus'),[36] there are also many in everyday speech. We speak of 'nameless fear' (i.e. an uncontrollable fear or anxiety), or 'ineffable wretchedness' (*Elend*); when we want to concretize an abstraction, we say 'namely'. There are taboo expressions—'do not mention it', 'speak of the devil', 'uncalled for', and so on. The root meaning of the German word for idea or concept (*Begriff*) is to 'grasp' (*greifen*). Even today words can become 'magic words'.

This numinous quality of names and words occurs in law as well. The 'right to one's name' is the classic 'right of personality' in German law (§12 BGB). We speak of an agent as acting 'in the name of another' (§164 BGB): by invoking the other person's name the law gains power over the principal—he is brought into the legal relationship. So, too, in expressions such as 'in the name of the law' or 'in the name of the people' (§311 par. 1 ZPO). France has the 'société anonyme', the Netherlands the 'naamloze vennootschap'.

5. LANGUAGE AS HERMENEUTIC

Furthermore, language is not only a method of denotation but also a means of learning. The everyday 'Say it in your own words' shows that to say something in our own words makes it our intellectual property. So, too, *discimus docendo*, we learn by teaching. Language is a complex of ideas which makes it possible to think and learn about the world: 'Language is a perpetual Orphic song | Which rules with Daedal harmony a throng | Of thoughts and forms, which else | Senseless and shapeless were.'[37] 'Different languages are like prisms variously angled, through which speakers see the world, each one differently.'[38]

Thus it is through language that we recognize and order

[36] Ibid.

[37] Shelley, *Prometheus Unbound*, iv. 415–17.

[38] Neumann-Duesberg (above n. 7) 42.

the world around us. The Bible tells us so, as we now realize: the first words of God create light ('fiat lux').[39] Language makes it possible to *see* the world! Indeed according to Wittgenstein 'the limits of language (*the* language I understand) mean the limits of *my* world'.[40] This is certainly true of legal concepts: they are 'a mental device to enable the mind to comprehend what it sees'.[41] Language is thus a 'world picture given form', as Gottfried Benn suggests in his poem *Worte*: 'Alone: really alone—just you and words.'

6. LAW AS THE CREATURE OF LANGUAGE

The constitutive and cognitive power of language is especially significant for law, for only in language do the concepts of positive law have any being at all. 'It is on the loom of language that all law is spun.'[42] Actual legislation, at any rate, is 'tied to language',[43] though with customary law the matter is more complicated, as we shall see. Such legal concepts and ideas have no counterpart in the real world, and generally cannot be represented without language. Language itself teaches us as much, for law 'wird gesprochen', we deliver 'verdicts' (telling the truth—'verum dicere') and have 'jurisdiction' (from 'ius dicere', speaking the law, as also in 'judicature', and the Latin 'iudex' and 'iudicium').

Law is more closely linked to language than are other literary or linguistic products. Ideas in other contexts are commonly expressed in language, but in law we are dealing with true concepts. An idea can be presented in many different ways, but legal concepts have quite precise linguistic

[39] Gen. 1: 3.

[40] Wittgenstein, *Tractatus Logico-Philosophicus*, prop. 5. 62 (Cambridge, 1933).

[41] Gobble, 'Nature, Man and Law', in Henson (ed.), *Landmarks of Law* 24, 36 (Boston, 1960).

[42] Weeremantry, *The Law in Crisis* 133 (London, 1975). He proceeds: 'Logic and History, morality and philosophy, commerce and science may each contribute threads of their own, but through the loom they must pass before they enter the fabric of the law.'

[43] Neumann-Duesberg (above n. 7) 27.

contours.[44] This sheds a new light on 'Begriffsjuriprudenz' or the jurisprudence of concepts, the conceptualism so despised today, and suggests a new approach to the formalism of ancient German law, when special formulae must be used and any mistake was fatal (whereas today we hold that *falsa demonstratio non nocet*). Perhaps behind it lies the sense that 'when words fail, no law remains'.

Something of this underlies §53 HGB, which provides that agency (*Prokura*) must be conferred expressly: no word, no representation. No word, no official either, unless on appointment the words 'acceptance into the office' are used;[45] without 'I swear' there is no oath.[46] The word 'Wechsel' is needed to make an instrument negotiable (art. 1 no. 1 WG). The power of language is clear when we can avoid the invalidity of a pledge without possession simply by calling it a 'transfer of security': all is well, the legal transaction is in order. Mere play with words? Mere spells?

We speak rather of 'canonical forms of words', of 'constitutive' or 'effective' speech acts.[47] All declarations in legal transactions are of this kind. Indeed the German word for legal transaction or act-in-law (*Rechtsgeschäft*) tells us as much, though we do not notice it: it combines the root meaning of 'Recht' (see below) and the normal meaning of 'Geschäft', from 'schaffen', to create or make. It replaced the Latin 'negotium', originally meaning 'activity' or 'business' (from 'nec otium', not at leisure).

I do not go so far as to say that there can be no law without language, for there exist certain taboos often not expressed in words which do and should constrain our conduct. Then again customary law is often inexplicit, not formulated in words but immanent in the facts themselves.[48]

[44] Marasinghe, 'Some Problems' (above n. 8) 515.

[45] §6 par. 2 BBG: 'unter Uebernahme in das Beamtenverhältnis'.

[46] §66 c par. 1 and 2 StPO, §481 par. 1 and 2 ZPO.

[47] Austin, *How to Do Things with Words* (2nd edn., Cambridge, Mass., 1975); Searle, *Speech Acts* (Cambridge, Mass., 1969); Searle, *Expression and Meaning* (Cambridge, Mass., 1979).

[48] Lon Fuller, *Anatomy of the Law* 44 (New York, 1968).

Even so, it is clear beyond a peradventure that in our verbally orientated culture the link between language and law is extremely close: each affects the other. That is enough for our purposes.

7. THE ETYMOLOGY OF LEGAL EXPRESSIONS

It is interesting to go into the etymological connections between words such as Recht and Sprache, lex and lingua, law and language, nomos and logos. It is already suggestive that 'lex' meaning 'law' appears in 'lexicon' as meaning 'word'. Their common root (legein) denotes 'speak' as well as other things.[49] A cognate root gives us 'logos' which, significantly enough, means both 'thought' (as in 'logic') and 'word'.[50] The parallel between 'lex'—'legein'—'logos' and 'law'—'speaking'—'thought/word' surely demonstrates the deep interfusion of law, speech, and thought. Another such parallel is between 'Satz'—'Satzung'—'Gesetz' and the Greek 'thesis' (Satz)—'themis' (Satzung, Gesetz). The inner relationship between 'Rede' (speech) and 'Recht' is reflected in 'redlich' (properly) and 'rechtlich' (rightly). The words 'mallus' and 'Mahlstatt' (court = Gericht) also have roots in words for speech, speaking, and talking (mahla, mapljan, mahalen); this family of words also exemplifies the inner connection between law and speech/language. Again the word 'domjan', a 'specialist legal term' in Gothic, developed in meaning from 'believe' through 'assert' to 'judge'. The Old German equivalent is 'toumen', which one can compare with the English 'doom', meaning judgement: doomsday is the Day of the Last Judgement; Domesday Book is the Last Word of the highest authority, the national land register.

The Greek word 'nomos' (law) also has remarkable connections. It is cognate with 'nemein' (to attribute), and cousin to the German words 'nehmen' (to take), 'vernehmen'

[49] *OED*.

[50] Ibid. Cf. Heidegger, *Sein und Zeit* 32 (8th edn., Tübingen, 1957). Much the same is true of 'raison'—'reason': *OED*.

(to perceive), and 'Vernunft' (reason). The word 'norm' leads us through 'gnosis' (the process of learning) and 'gnarus' (knowledgeable) to 'narrare' (to relate). The Latin words 'fas' and 'nefas' (for what is divinely permitted or prohibited), like 'phami' in Doric Greek and 'fari' in Latin (to speak), go back to the Indo-Germanic root 'bha-' (to speak). Similarly the Greek 'dikaion' (law, what is laid down) and 'dike' (what is ethical or right) are apparently connected with the Latin 'dicere' (to speak).

The German word for law, 'Recht', also has overtones of the creation myth, through 'richten', to put to rights, 'errichten', to construct, cognate with the English 'wright', which designates the constructive workman, the creator.[51] This overtone of meaning can be heard when we say that God will 'put it right' (richten). Similarly the word for the German lay judge of the Middle Ages, 'Schöffe', goes back to 'schaffen' and 'erschaffen', to create. The word 'rechtsschöpferisch', creative of law, is thus basically tautologous. We have come full circle.

These roots are doubtless to be explained on the basis that language had to develop before rules could arise or be made. The first abstract laws a child learns are the laws of speech. Language becomes the model of structuring, and this leaves its mark; so law becomes shaped by language and the idea of law-in-words, legislation, arises. It is easy to conclude that positive law, legislation, can be understood as an idea created by language or manifested in it, that law is a great social system of speech and communication. These considerations must suffice as an introduction to the mystery of language, for it is its effect on law which is our subject-matter.

8. LANGUAGE AND THOUGHT

'At the pinnacle of all civilization stands a miracle: language', as Jacob Burkhardt said.[52] Again he said 'Man has

[51] *OED*.

[52] Jakob Burckhardt, *Über das Studium der Geschichte* 276 (ed. Ganz, Munich, 1982).

as many hearts as he has languages'.[53] The effect of a people's language on its cultural history is 'enormous'. The point is implicit that language influences thought.

This hardly surprises the lawyer. He knows that the deaf-and-dumb have diminished responsibility in civil law, and in criminal law as it used to be.[54] The poet knows it too. Schiller wrote of 'a developed language that composes and thinks for you'.[55] And we know from everyday experience that the clearer our style, the clearer our thinking.

Language and thought form a unit, the strength of the spoken form is as that of the thought itself.[56] Our own experience tells us of the spiritual energy of language: speaking fuels our thinking. For example, if we are unsure of the exact words of a poem or song we only need to start reciting it, and it carries us along by itself. Again, when we make up jingles at parties the rhymes at our disposal stimulate the train of thought. Speech has a magnetic effect on our thinking.

Here we approach the philosophy of language of Johann Gottfried von Herder[57] and Wilhelm von Humboldt.[58] For Humboldt language is the formative organ of thought. It is not just a device for representing the truth, but 'much more, of discovering truth hitherto unrecognised'. Different languages represent different world-views. When we learn another language we unconsciously adopt its speakers' world of thought: 'Language thinks in us'.[59] Similar views are held by Weisgerber[60] and de Saussure.[61]

[53] Ibid. at 276 n. 3.

[54] §828 par. 2 sent. 2 BGB, and previous §55 StGB.

[55] Schiller, *Dilettant* in *Tabulae Votivae*, 1 *Werke* 319 (Salzburg, 1952); see also Heinrich von Kleist, 'Über die allmähliche Verfertigung der Gedanken beim Reden', in 2 *Sämtliche Werke und Briefe* 319 (6th edn., Munich, 1947).

[56] Cardozo, 'Law and Literature', in *Selected Writings of Benjamin Nathan Cardozo* 339, 340 (New York, 1947).

[57] Herder, *Abhandlung über den Ursprung der Sprache* (Berlin, 1972).

[58] Wilhelm von Humboldt, *Über die Verschiedenheit des menschlichen Sprachbaues und ihren Einfluss auf die geistige Entwicklung des Menschengeschlechts* (Berlin, 1836).

[59] Wezel, *Sprache und Geist* iv (Leipzig, 1935); Holldack (above n. 1) 83.

[60] Weisgerber, *Von den Kräften der deutschen Sprache* (Düsseldorf, 1962).

[61] De Saussure, *Cours de linguistique générale* (Paris, 1915); for appraisal, see Greenberg, 'Concerning Inferences from Linguistic to Nonlinguistic Data', in Hoijer

Language plugs us into a formal canon fixed ages ago; it constitutes the structure of human intelligence. Language gives us a world-view which has developed through time, the 'world-view developed by that language-community.' Language has 'the character of a world-view', is a 'shaped world-view'.[62] We take our world-view for granted as the product of our natural sane common sense, but in reality it is provided by our mother tongue.[63] 'Vox populi, vox dei' (vox!) is here suggestive.

Language guides our thinking along particular lines. We recall the regimentation of language, such as the terrifying Newspeak in George Orwell's *1984* which was designed 'to make all other modes of thought impossible': 'a heretical thought—that is, a thought diverging from the principles of Ingsoc—should be literally unthinkable, at least so far as thought is dependent on words.'[64] (Ingsoc, or English Socialism, is the compulsory ideology of Orwell's state.)

9. THE PRINCIPLE OF RELATIVITY IN LANGUAGE

On groundwork done by Johann Gottfried von Herder, Wilhelm von Humboldt, and Edward Sapir,[65] the major contributor to the study of the effect on the structure of thought of the structure of language is Benjamin Lee Whorf.[66] The Whorfian hypothesis is that all thinking has a linguistic background.[67] Every language has a kind of logic, a general

(ed.), *Language in Culture* (Chicago, 1954); Brown & Lennerberg, 'A Study in Language and Cognition', 49 *J.Abnormal Psych.* 454 (1954).

[62] Neumann-Duesberg (above n. 7) 66, 72; see also Porzig, *Das Wunder der Sprache* 366 (Berne, 1950).

[63] Preceded in this by William of Ockham, according to Schlageter, 'Wilhelm von Occam', in Fries & Kretschmar, 1 *Klassiker der Theologie* 239, 240 (Munich, 1981).

[64] George Orwell, *1984*, 226 (New York, 1949).

[65] Sapir, 'The Status of Linguistics as a Science', in *Selected Writings of Edward Sapir in Language, Culture and Personality* (Berkeley, 1949).

[66] Whorf, 'Science and Linguistics', in Whorf, *Language, Thought, and Reality* 207, 214 (ed. Carroll, Cambridge, Mass., 1956); Whorf, 'Languages and Logic', ibid. 233, 239.

[67] Whorf, 'Language, Mind, and Reality', ibid. at 246, 247.

frame of reference, which shapes the thinking of its user. Man's thinking is guided by unknown linguistic mechanisms.

Every language is a vast pattern-system, different from others, in which are culturally ordained the forms and categories by which the personality not only communicates, but also analyzes nature, notices or neglects types of relationship and phenomena, channels his reasoning, and builds the house of his consciousness.[68]

Thus Whorf sees important connections between the grammar of a language and the general character of a culture—a kind of linguistic principle of relativity.

Whorf's views are not uncontested. Critics deny the probative value of his evidence, taken from the language of North American Indians.[69] They also object to his supposed assumption that there is no thought outside language, a view which Whorf does not actually assert.[70] Even Whorf's supporters admit that the connections he makes are often intuited rather than proved,[71] although some of his points are convincingly established.[72] The current view is that while the mind is not inextricably bound by language (as is shown by the existence of sub-languages such as mathematics,[73] accounting,[74] or 'Pascal') yet the gravitational pull of language is such that little can escape it. A moderate answer consistent with the present state of research is as follows: 'A person's thinking is "relative" to the expressive possibilities of a language-system and its semantic structures in the sense that

[68] Ibid. at 252. Cf. Popper & Eccles, *The Self and Its Brain* (Berlin, 1977); Adam Schaff, *Language and Connaissance* (Paris, 1965).

[69] Noda (ed. Dil), *Language Structure and Translation* 184 (Stanford, 1975); Weinstein, *The Civic Tongue: The Political Consequences of Language Choices* 19 (New York, 1983).

[70] Vendler, 'Wordless Thought', in McCormack & Wurm (eds.), *Language and Thought, Anthropological Issues* 29 (The Hague, 1977).

[71] Friedrich (ed. Dil), *Language, Context and the Imagination* 441, 446 (Stanford, 1979).

[72] Pirsig (above n. 19) 349 f.; see also Herrigel, *Zen in the Art of Archery* (New York, 1983).

[73] Compare the connections between the German 'Zahl' (number), 'zählen' (to count), 'erzählen' (to narrate), 'taal' (Dutch for 'speech'), and in English 'tally', 'tell', and 'tale'.

[74] Tanaka, *The Structure of Accounting Language* (Tokyo, 1982).

it can only take form by fitting itself to these given conditions. It is possible for higher-level abstract thought to emancipate itself from the common language by creating artificial symbol-systems, but thought can never become fully independent of language.'[75]

10. LANGUAGE AND VALUE-JUDGEMENTS

Language not only shapes the process of ratiocination: it also expresses value-judgements, as can be seen in such phrases as 'best butter', 'pure wool', 'people's democracy', 'plenary meeting'.[76] Language appraises the world and aligns the mind with its appraisals. The individual gets from language not only a way of putting the phenomena of the world into order, but also a scale of values and range of feelings. Language influences our sentiments and desires. 'Language is a sociopsychological force which determines both the rational and the irrational content of expression.'[77]

In addition to affecting the formal structures of thought, language also affects its subject-matter. Language determines what in any culture is to be treated as essential and what is not. This it does through the vocabulary it makes available, through its active and passive moods, and through its tenses: 'The individual who grows up in his mother tongue builds not only empty containers but also the intellectual content to fill them.'[78]

Because of the close connection between language and law, language is very much the decisive intellectual force in law. Law certainly uses language, but language is the stronger:[79] it is a formative influence on law, somewhat like geography—

[75] Gipper, *Gibt es ein sprachliches Relativitätsprinzip? Untersuchungen zur Sapir-Whorf-Hypothese* 248 (Frankfurt, 1972). See also Weinstein (above n. 69) 19.

[76] Neumann-Duesberg (above n. 7) 76; see also Lakoff & Johnson, *Metaphors We Live By* (Chicago, 1980).

[77] Neumann-Duesberg (above n. 7) 73–84.

[78] Ibid. at 82.

[79] Ibid. at 83.

indeed experts in linguistics use terms such as 'geography of legal words'[80] and 'geography of legal language'.[81]

II. EXAMPLES

The influence of language on law can be nicely seen in German and English. One material difference is that German, unlike English, is an inflected language: the ending of one word often depends on what word follows it, and the endings of sentences determine their meaning, whereas in English sense depends on word order. Again, German places the past participle at the end of the sentence and the verb at the end of a subordinate clause. These characteristics require that the sentence be thought out in advance: German syntax is a continuing education in forward planning, in organization. As to law, one should note that Latin was the language used until the nineteenth century, and the mode of legal thinking was also affected by the characteristics of that language, the 'logic of Latin' of which one sometimes speaks.

No wonder, then, that our law is more tightly constructed than English law, which strikes us as rather 'loose'. Perhaps this is because the notions we meet in English law, such as good faith, estoppel, trust, are rather vague, more open, less technically developed than ours. English statutes, on the other hand, go into enormous detail and are long and wearisome.

We should now understand why Noda begins his *Introduction to Japanese Law* with a description of the Japanese language.[82] Noda shows that European languages are more logical, that Japanese is better adapted to the expression of feeling than to logical argument; as a language of poetry rather than scholarship, it is not so good at

[80] Schmidt-Wiegand (ed.), *Studien zur historischen Rechtswortgeographie* (Munich, 1978).

[81] Von Künssberg, *Rechtssprachgeographie* (Heidelberg, 1926).

[82] Noda, *Introduction to Japanese Law* 9–13 (Tokyo, 1976); see also Angelo, 'Thinking of Japanese Law: A Linguistic Primer', 12 *Comp. & Int.L.J.S.Africa* 83 (1979).

expressing logical relations.[83] Others have put it laconically: 'Logic has no place in Japanese thought.'[84] Noda expressly confirms the linguists' theory that man's thought is shaped by the language in which it is expressed;[85] and when people reach the same conclusion from very different starting-points, that is good evidence for its correctness.

This brings us to another difference in the use of language, the difference between what is spoken and what is not. The tendency in our culture is to address matters explicitly, to speak out; in the United States the tendency is even stronger. In Japan, by contrast, we are told that the proportion of spoken to unspoken is 1 : 9. Of the iceberg of communication only the tip is spoken word. 'The general view is that the less verbal one's position is, the more polite and rich it is in implications.'[86] Similarly we are much readier to address questions directly rather than skirt them.

12. THE LESSONS FOR COMPARATIVE LAW

All this is very alarming for the comparative lawyer: if law lives in and through language, what happens to it when it is transferred into another language? If the structure of a language influences, or even determines, the mode and content of thought, might it not be that any language can only express certain thoughts, and that these thoughts differ from culture to culture? Indeed, one sometimes hears that it is simply not possible to find proper equivalents for the central expressions of a culture. We must certainly take account of this on the basis of present findings; for the limits of speech often mark the limits of our understanding.[87]

[83] Noda (above n. 82) 12.

[84] Kim & Lawson, 'The Law of the Subtle Mind', 28 *I.C.L.Q.* 21 (1979); Noda, 'La conception du droit des japonais', in *Études juridiques Julliot de la Morandière* 421 (Paris, 1964).

[85] Noda (above n. 82) 13, citing de Saussure (above n. 61) 155; Jean Stoetzel, *La psychologie sociale* 130 f. (Paris, 1963).

[86] Yotsukura, 'Ethnolinguistic Introduction to Japanese Literature', in McCormack & Wurm (eds.) (above n. 70) 261, 263.

[87] Wittgenstein (above n. 40) prop. 7: 'Whereof one cannot speak, thereof one must be silent.'

Could it be the case that certain legal ideas are insusceptible of satisfactory translation into another language, that they are inevitably altered in the process? 'Fair' may not mean quite the same thing in England and in Germany. Furthermore, when a rule is taken over it enters a different context of discourse whose independent speech-dynamic may influence the meaning and deflect the idea in an unexpected direction.[88] For example, the new German Law of Accounting translates the English 'true and fair view' as 'ein den tatsächlichen Verhältnissen entsprechendes Bild',[89] which hardly does the impossible of catching all the nuance of the English expression, with its subtly subjective and less factual value-judgements.

If this question has not seemed too acute hitherto, this is because comparative law has always concentrated on systems in Indo-Germanic languages,[90] a situation which is rapidly changing. And even within the Indo-Germanic family there are difficulties. Just try to translate such English notions as 'chose in action', 'fee simple', 'feoffee', 'domicile', or, as above 'true and fair view'![91]

Admittedly we cannot measure the influence of language precisely in any particular case,[92] nor does the structure of language explain everything about law: no formal structure can cage the truth of life. Language is one factor among others, and there are human elements common to all cultures[93] and languages, a universal deep structure for human

[88] According to Frege, *Die Grundlagen der Arithmetik* 73 (Breslau, 1884), words have meaning only in the context of a sentence. See also Hart, *Essays on Bentham* 10 (Oxford, 1982); Wittgenstein (above n. 40) prop. 3. 3, 3. 3. 4. This is relevant to the relationship between legal idea and language. See Holldack (above n. 1) 84 ff.

[89] §264 par. 2 HGB, new version.

[90] Whorf, *Science and Linguistics* (above n. 66) 214.

[91] Examples from Marasinghe, *Some Problems* (above n. 8). See also Steiner, 'The Problems of Legal Translation', in Banakas (ed.), *United Kingdom Law in the 1980s* 259 (London, 1988).

[92] Paul Henle, 'Language, Thought and Culture', in Henle (ed.), *Language, Thought and Culture* 1 (Ann Arbor, 1958).

[93] Llompart, 'Rechtsbewusstsein', 14 *Rechtstheorie* 285 (1983); Mubirumusoke, 'Application of the Received Law of Torts in East Africa and the Problem of Transplanting Legal Norms', in Bechtler (ed.), *Liber Amicorum Honoring Prof. Lon F. Fuller* 127, 187 (Deventer, 1978).

grammar,[94] which muffle its differential effects. So while the relativity of language makes the comparatist's task harder, it need not make it impossible. 'Relativity' does not mean 'determinism', and the obstacles it poses can be overcome.[95]

But if comparative lawyers are to make any contribution to our own law, they must act responsibly and attend closely to the connections between language and law. Legal linguistics is an essential concomitant of comparative law, one which does not make it any easier.

13. CONSEQUENCES FOR THE AUTHORITY OF LAW

The idea of a uniform deep structure for all human grammar leads to problems which go far beyond comparative law, but it also brings us back to the starting-point of our reflections. According to Chomsky people are born with this deep structure embedded into them, they are programmed with it; it is a 'proto-human-grammar' from which are developed all human grammars as we know them.[96]

While the details of Chomsky's theory are contested, the close relationship of language and law prompts us to ask whether anything of the sort could be true of law as well. Perrott believes that certain legal ideas might be genetically transmitted, 'natural law in the DNA-code'.[97] The various systems of positive law would be developments from this.[98] He concludes:

> On this view, the various positive law systems are differing surface manifestations of the underlying deep structure of law . . . If this were the case, the deep structure of law would impose on all humans certain rather abstractly stated duties, and these duties would be 'Fundamental Duties' in an ultimate sense.[99]

[94] Chomsky, *Language and Mind* 76 (2nd edn., New York, 1972).

[95] Gipper (above n. 75) 248; Weinstein (above n. 69) 32.

[96] Chomsky, (above n. 94), reviewed by Skinner, 'Verbal Behaviour', 35 *Language* 26 (1969); appraisal in Lyons, *Noam Chomsky* (New York, 1970).

[97] Perrott, 'Has Law a Deep Structure? The Origin of Fundamental Duties', in Lasok, Jaffey, Perrott, & Sachs, *Fundamental Duties* at 1, 3 (Oxford, 1980).

[98] Ibid. at 7.

[99] Ibid. at 10.

This theory sheds a new light on natural law, on the sense of justice, on the 'instinct for law'. So, too, on Goethe's reference to 'the law innate in us' (above p. 44).

We cannot pursue the theory here, but if the fundaments of language are genetically structured, it must be the same with law, by reason of language's influence on it. There would then be a genetically transmitted structure of law through the medium of language, which would diminish the differences between legal systems which are due to the superficially different structures of their languages.

But on another relevant point there is general agreement, namely that our feeling for play, rhythm, and proportion is inborn. How else could one account for the universal acceptance of the beauty of the Golden Section?[100] This predilection for rhythm and proportion is culturally reflected in alliteration and rhyme, ludic features which touch the very root and core of our being.

This insight tells us something about the reason for the validity, the authority of law. Legal language causes a response in our very selves, is on our spiritual wave-length. We have in ourselves a receiver on the same wave-length as the sender of legal language. Much as music pulls us along, as soldiers march to the beat of the drum, so we are captivated by the structure, rhythm, and sound of legal language. (There are classical instances of its good and bad effects, bad in *The Pied Piper of Hamelin* and good in Grimm's *The Singing Bone* and *Van den Machandelboom*.)

These almost magical qualities enhance the efficacy of the legal rule. Language uses the cultural sensibility we have inherited with our genes; we obey the law from a consensual, inner impulse which we experience as moral duty, even as joy. Law resonates within us, is our own; we now want to do what we should do because we are in harmony with it. No free legal system can get on without this.

Now we understand better why ancient law so often took

[100] 1 : 1·618.

the form of poetry. An oral legal tradition is naturally more sensitive to language. And where the power of enforcement is weak, it is all the more important that subjects of law be convinced of its merits and eager to bear their part.[101] Poetry can bring this about by deploying the spiritual power of the word.[102] We can tell this from the songs of the church: their primary function is not confessional but to instil belief, to lead to faith.[103] If, as happens too often today, the law does not appeal to our feeling for language, we find it alien, a flood of rules breaking over us. Unless great care is taken with language the positive law will awaken no sense of its justice.

[101] Hagerström, *Inquiries into the Nature of Law and Morals* 130 (Stockholm, 1903).

[102] Dilcher, *Paarformeln in der Rechtssprache des frühen Mittelalters* 15 (Darmstadt, 1961); see also Huizinga, *Homo Ludens* 5, 75, 125, 229 (Amsterdam, 1939).

[103] Compare 'Thy statutes have been my songs in the house of my pilgrimage', Ps. 119: 57; Danet, *The Magic Flute: A Prosodic Analysis of Binominal Expressions in Legal Hebrew*, Text 4 143 (1984); Bydlinsky, 'Rechtsgesinnung als Aufgabe', in *Festschrift Larenz zum 80. Geburtstag* 1 (Munich, 1983); Erik Wolf, 'Verpflichtende Sprache im Rechtsdenken', in Erik Wolf, *Studien zur Geschichte des Rechtsdenkens* 215 (Frankfurt, 1982).

14

Religion and Law

Religion is another factor which comparatists must take very seriously, but the close bond between religion and law is so generally recognized that I can deal with it fairly briefly. Our normal response is to point to the special category of 'religious legal systems', including Islamic law, Mosaic law, Hindu law, and canon law. We do not see our own law as falling in any such category.

In a purely technical sense this is correct enough, since unlike the systems mentioned above our law applies to people independently of their religious belief. But if we take the question more broadly ours is an unsatisfactory response, at any rate for the comparative lawyer. We need not broach the question whether law can exist at all without religion, or at any rate some metaphysical basis.[1] Harold J. Berman has recently denied it. For him, law is dead without religion or some substitute therefor.[2] Others reject this view on the ground that mutuality or reciprocity (*do ut des*) is the basis of all law.[3] I myself agree with Pannenberg, who takes an intermediate view which does justice to both anthropological and religious aspects:

> The first point of view explains the wide spread of broadly similar views of law in human communities with divergent religious persuasions. The second view does justice to the equally widespread conviction that traditional ethics are of divine origin and are traceable to the (divine) creator of the universe and society.[4]

[1] See Pennock & Chapman (eds.), *Religion, Morality and the Law* (New York, 1988); Denning, *The Changing Law* 99 (London, 1953); Dawson, *Religion and Culture* 155 (New York, 1948); Alexander Beck, *Itinera Juris* 13, 29 (Berne, 1980). Basic is Maine, *Ancient Law* (London, 1865).

[2] Harold J. Berman, *The Interaction of Law and Religion* 73 f. (Nashville, 1974); Berman, 'The Religious Foundations of Western Law', 24 *Cath.U.L.Rev.* 490 (1975).

[3] Nowell-Smith, 'Religion and Morality', in 7 *Encyclopedia of Philosophy* 150, 151, 155 (1967); Diamond, *Primitive Law* (London, 1935).

[4] Pannenberg, 'Christliche Rechtsbegründung', in *Handbuch der Christlichen Ethik* 323 (2nd edn., Freiburg, 1979).

At any rate it is clear—and that is enough for our purposes—that social norms have in the past been based on religion (or some positive inner faith) and to some extent are still so based today.

If we look at our law with this in mind we will find a mass of religious traits, centring on basic rights, equality, contract law,[5] good *faith*, family law, and the law of inheritance. The Bible has left its mark on our law thanks to the Judaeo-Christian tradition,[6] and especially Christian thought.[7] 'The Church taught the West what a modern legal system should be.'[8] Our law in the West was cradled in the church,[9] and canon law played an important role in the reception,[10] for it was the filter of Christian faith that determined which portions of Roman law should be adopted and which should not. In the heyday of secular humanism the role of Christianity was sometimes underplayed,[11] less because there was any doubt about the facts than on the basis that 'what should not have happened could not have happened'.[12] Certainly Eastern observers say that Western law is incomprehensible unless Christianity is taken into account: religion is the key to understanding the essence of Western law.[13]

[5] Berman, *The Interaction* (above n. 2) 60; Berman, *Justice in the U.S.S.R.* 183 (Cambridge, Mass., 1981).

[6] Ehrlich, *The Holy Bible and the Law* (New York, 1962); Haim-Cohn, 'Prolegomenon to the Theory and History of Jewish Law', in Newman (ed.), *Essays in Jurisprudence in Honor of Roscoe Pound* 44 (Indianapolis, 1962); Jackson, *Jewish Law in Legal History and the Modern World* (Leiden, 1980).

[7] Berman, 'Theological Sources of the Western Legal Tradition', 46 *Revista U. Puerto Rico* 371 (1979); Berman, *Law and Revolution: The Formation of Western Legal Tradition* (Cambridge, Mass., 1983).

[8] Berman, *The Interaction* (above n. 2) 59.

[9] Berman, *The Religious Foundations* (above n. 2) 491; Carlton & Hayes, *Christianity and Western Civilization* (Stanford, 1954).

[10] Wieacker, *Privatrechtsgeschichte der Neuzeit* 71 (2nd edn., Göttingen, 1967).

[11] Melinck, 'Secularism in the Law: The Religion of Secular Humanism', 8 *Ohio N.U.L.Rev.* 329 (1981).

[12] Berman, *The Religious Foundations* (above n. 2); Berman, 'The Influence of Christianity upon the Development of Law', 12 *Okla.L.Rev.* 86 (1959); Stumpff, 'Theology and Jurisprudence', 10 *Vand.L.Rev.* 885 (1957).

[13] Angelo, 'Thinking of Japanese Law: A Linguistic Primer', 12 *Comp. & Int.L.J.S.Africa* 83 (1979).

This finding is important for comparative lawyers, for they must inquire whether a legal institution can be prised from one religious context and set in another, and how it might be altered by the change of religious environment. This investigation is still in its infancy. It is to be borne in mind that religion often achieves its influence on law through the realm of morals, where it is king. The different morals associated with a different religion can reinforce a legal rule or sap it of all efficacy. Take the example of divorce. One can import divorce law from one system to another and still have very different rates of divorce. This is an area where prognosis is extremely difficult.

15

Conclusion

Here we must end. The considerations in these final chapters may not have any immediate bearing on the actual thinking or conduct of legal practitioners, yet they seem to me to be important, for they show how our law, our doctrine, and our way of applying it are all dependent on our culture. They demonstrate how our professional life is conditioned by geography, language, and religion, and indicate that our legal thinking has a framework of which we are generally unconscious. When we become aware of these factors and formulate them, consequences are bound to ensue, even if we cannot tell precisely what. This shows the power of comparative law.

I was to have given you some concrete instances of the impact of comparative law on our own legal system here in Germany, with emphasis on demonstrable practical results. But a professor cannot change his spots, and it has all become rather theoretical. Yet I must in conclusion say something practical even if it is only loosely connected with doctrine and lawyering, something one has to know in order to understand the appeal of comparative law.

In demonstrating the influences to which our law is subject, comparative law opens our eyes ('it is like escaping from prison into the open air'),[1] it stimulates thought, it gives us new arguments, it stirs the imagination. It informs us of new developments, and in breaking the bounds of 'provincial jurisprudence' makes legal science universal once more.[2] It was from the United States that we first learnt that to be born might constitute an actionable harm, and doubtless in

[1] Lawson, 'Comparative Law, Instrument of Legal Culture' in Lawson, 2 *Many Laws: Selected Essays* 68 (Amsterdam, 1977).

[2] Von Jhering, 1 *Geist des römischen Rechts auf den verschiedenen Stufen seiner Entwicklung* 15 (10th edn., Aalen, 1968).

this promiscuous age we shall soon learn to deal with liability for spreading AIDS, inside marriage or out. Comparatists hear of new cases before they have arisen at home.

Comparative law thus serves as an international seismograph, as an early warning system; it is an excellent means of learning about impending social change. Foreign law often reflects world-wide tendencies which will be felt here sooner or later, and comparative law can often teach us what we have to look forward to, what problems may be about to present themselves in legal guise. The ability of a legal system to react to change depends in part on its ability to make good use of the experiences of other systems.[3] Despite their cultural differences, all the peoples of the world are in the same boat, and with every technological improvement in travel and communication that boat is getting smaller. We must realize how our legal thinking is affected by international trends, as regards private radio and commercial television, for example, or electronics in law (and here I must refer again to the dependence of law on language). In this way we discover not only the defects of our legal institutions, but also their merits; we come to appreciate the inestimable value of the legacy of Roman law and the systematics of the BGB, and we can see the real utility of clear concepts and our ingenious land register.

This should enable and encourage us to accept responsibility for our own legal culture, for the cultural identity of our law is indeed our responsibility, and we must not let comparative law turn it into a patchwork. Comparative law is of great practical use when it is necessary to defend ourselves against the imperialism of other systems, such as overextensive doctrines of jurisdiction, anti-trust law,[4] and foreign rules about embargoes.

But comparative law has a more important role, which it

[3] Touster, 'Reflections on the Émigré Scholar: In Memory of Arthur Lenhoff', 16 *Buffalo L.Rev.* (1966–7); Fuller, *The Principles of Social Order* 296 (Durham, NC, 1981).

[4] Grossfeld & Rogers, 'A Shared Values Approach in International Economic Law', 22 *I.C.L.Q.* 931 (1983).

is increasingly playing: it equips us to be ambassadors of our own legal culture, to show it in its proper light.[5] It relieves us of the aridity of national self-contemplation, shows us how it may be misunderstood abroad, and helps us to reach the foreign ear. But this is only possible if we have some idea (more is hardly ever possible) of the cultural background of the foreign law. By the same token employment abroad will be more readily available for the young lawyers we train.

This leads to the question of 'law and developing countries'. We should not to be too eager to teach other countries what to do. We learn from comparative law that every culture has a rationality of its own, it need not adopt ours. If we remember this, we can forget jokes about Eskimos trying to teach pygmies how to cope with the heat of the jungle.

It is even more in our own interest to keep our system approachable and comprehensible, especially at a time of increasing unification of law, internationalization of standards, and creation of general principles of law. Our future depends on it. Comparative law is a constant reminder that these tasks are literally essential, and must be taken very seriously. If our legal culture is to retain its significance we must use comparative law to help us meet these challenges. Our generation will be judged by how well it performs this task.

Our great predecessors have set us a daunting standard. Mittermaier has a really remarkable international reputation; Savigny had immense influence in England through his pupil Vinogradov and Vinogradov's friend, Maitland;[6] so, too, did Jhering and Ehrlich in the United States[7] through Holmes[8] and Roscoe Pound.[9] Then there is Rabel, whose books had an enormous effect abroad;[10] one need only mention his influence on Llewellyn and thus on the Uniform Commercial

[5] Murphy, 'The Diminishing World of Western Law', 16 *Texas Int'l L.J.* (1981).

[6] H. A. L. Fisher, *Frederic W. Maitland* 18 (Cambridge, 1910).

[7] See generally, McDonnell & Manson, *Great Jurists of the World* (Boston, 1914).

[8] Howe, *Justice Oliver Wendell Holmes* 150, 204 (Cambridge, Mass., 1963).

[9] Pound, *Outlines of Lectures on Jurisprudence* 16, 32 (5th edn., Cambridge, Mass., 1943); Pound, *Jurisprudence* (5 vols., St Paul, 1959).

[10] Rabel, *Das Recht des Warenkaufs* (Berlin, 1937); Rabel, *The Conflict of Laws* (Ann Arbor, 1945–58).

Code.[11] The names of Kelsen and Radbruch are world-famous, and we must mention the emigrants from Germany and Austria such as Rheinstein, Kahn-Freund, Kronstein, Ehrenzweig, Kessler, Friedmann, Werner Goldschmidt, Martin Wolf, Nussbaum, Lipstein, Riesenfeld, and Lenhoff.[12] In praising Sohm's *Institutions of Roman Law* Holmes[13] told the budding American lawyer to 'Read the works of the great German jurists, and see how much more the world is governed today by Kant than by Bonaparte'.[14] There is food for thought!

When Rabel refounded his *Zeitschrift für ausländisches und internationales Privatrecht* in 1949 he said in the Foreword: 'After such fearful turmoil it is more than ever important that the West consolidate its powers to build law. We must attack with renewed vigour the task of ironing out needless differences, of simplifying international trade and improving the systems of private law.' The same is true today.

Yet comparative law has dangerous temptations as well as blessings ('the air of the great wide world'). It must be handled with sobriety. The comparatist should note and apply the words of Zuckmayer: 'Half of life is good luck, the other half discipline. The second is the more important half, since without discipline one's good luck does one no good.' We must be mindful of the limits of comparative law, but go as far as we can with self-confidence and courage. We must weigh up the good and bad, for only by recognizing the weakness of comparative law can we learn its true worth. When we have reached our limits we shall appreciate the grandeur of our subject, the miracle of law, and wonder at it. W. H. Auden put it most tenderly in his poem *Law Like Love*, which concludes

[11] Herman, 'Llewellyn the Civilian: Speculations on the Contribution of Continental Experience to the Uniform Commercial Code', 56 *Tul.L.Rev.* 1125 (1982); Whitman, 'Commercial Law and the American Volk: A Note on Llewellyn's German Sources for the Uniform Commercial Code', 97 *Yale L.J.* 156 (1987).

[12] Lewis A. Coser, *Refugee Scholars in America: Their Impact and Their Experiences* (New Haven, 1984).

[13] Holmes, 'The Path of the Law', 10 *Harv.L.Rev.* 457, 476, 478 (1897).

[14] 15 *RabelsZ* 1 (1949–50).

Like love we don't know where or why,
Like love we can't compel or fly,
Like love we often weep,
Like love we seldom keep.[15]

For me the greatest value of comparative law lies in the deeper insight it gives into the phenomenon of law itself. This is the greatest contribution it can make to German law, but I cannot tell you quite how it is achieved. So while it remains an open question what the effect of comparative law on German law may be, the future is ours only if we accept the challenge of comparative law with a full understanding of both its strength and its weakness.

[15] W. H. Auden, *Collected Poems* 208 (London, 1976).

Index